SETTLING ESTATES

IN NORTH CAROLINA

A
Step-By-Step
Guide

Jane J. Young

ISBN 1-878086-83-9

Library of Congress Control Number
00 133353

Printed in the United States of America

Book design by Elizabeth House
Cover design by Beth Hennington

Down Home Press
P.O. Box 4126
Asheboro, N.C. 27204

Distributed by John F. Blair, Publisher, 1406 Plaza Dr., Winston-Salem, N.C. 27103

Foreword

Why did a woman whose primary work had been that of nurturer and teacher of children decide to write a book about estate settlement? Actually, the book was not conceived by intent.

An aunt of mine who lived in Randleman died in 1984. Her long and devastating battle with MLS joined with other conditions to take a heavy toll on my uncle. He was no longer able to organize, keep records, do work that had to be done. He and my aunt had no children. I was placed by circumstance into the position of primary responsibility for beginning my aunt's estate work.

I had no previous experience, but finding a certificate of deposit in a pile of trash on the back porch and a sizable check in a stack of newspapers on the kitchen cabinet taught me my first lesson: thoroughness is essential. Two handwritten wills turned up, and they designated my uncle as executor. The nature of the wills and the nature of my uncle constituted, even to the inexperienced, a clear mandate: find a lawyer.

I made an appointment, gathered my uncle and everything else that looked at all significant (including an array of church envelope corners taped around coins gathered from many purses) and headed for the lawyer's office. There, I dumped everything except Uncle Gene on the secretary's desk. She looked more than a little startled, but she responded tactfully — and I began learning about inventories.

During the two years it took to complete the settlement, I escorted Gene on all the necessary rounds to banks, S&L's, lawyer's office, etc. The time with him was time I came to treasure.

He was a gentleman and a gentle man, a poet by nature. He often couldn't remember what day it was, but he could still quote, with faultless memory, poems many pages long. Getting him started on a first line was like pressing the "on" button on a tape player. I can still hear his voice reciting "The Ballad of Dan McGrew" and "When Earth's Last Picture Is Painted." One day he surprised me with two poems that must have been stored in his mind during much earlier days — one about an outhouse, the other about "things I learned from women."

As he and I listened to all the explanations by various bank and S&L employees, I was beginning to learn, from them, about estate accounts. Uncle Gene's most frequent comment about the whole process was, "I didn't know it was so complicated to die."

I agreed. I felt as though I were in a maze and had to wait at every turn for someone to tell me where to set my foot. In addition to that, some of the words that were supposed to explain to me what the attorney or his secretary would do and what my uncle and I should do seemed to be words I was supposed to understand but did not.

I had never heard of letters testamentary; the word "probate" could have been Arabic for all it clarified for me. What were those "fiduciary" taxes the attorney had mentioned?

Sometimes I clearly understood "what" but not "why." Why was it that we needed to do whatever it was the lawyer had said do? Even when someone was telling me which way to turn, I still felt insecure.

I was embarrassed that I had to keep asking questions about what I felt I should understand, but didn't. Dealing with my forgetful uncle and his confused niece must have been a real ordeal for that law office. I will have to say they helped us with considerable grace. I was especially grateful for the straightforward but patient manner with which both the attorney and his secretary tried to communicate with Gene.

One important lesson for me, however, resulted from some stress in that relationship. I learned there are important questions a prospective client should ask before work begins.

In 1986, my husband and I moved his parents into our home to care for his terminally ill mother. When she died, her estate went to my father-in-law.

Entire estate to the spouse is the simplest settlement, and that was fortunate. Pop was 86 and ... um ... frugal. He would never have seen the sense in paying a lawyer, no matter what was involved. He wasn't, however, able to negotiate the process on his own. He was quite alert, but not an organizer or record keeper, and he didn't know what the process entailed.

We had moved from Waynesville to Gastonia just four months earlier, and my husband's new job was extremely time consuming. The move and Mom's illness had extracted me from the classroom, so I began working with estate number two.

Pop had a quick and unique sense of humor that made him fun to be with and often cast new light on the mundane. "How did you sleep last night?" my husband asked him one morning. "Frequently," Pop responded.

Interestingly, he, too, was a poet. He wrote poems as well as quoting the works of others. His favorite lines were from Sidney Lanier's "The Marshes of Glynn." This gentle man, however, also had a strong will — and working with him was a different kind of adventure.

He wasn't fond of being told what he had to do. Neither did he put much stock in systems or schedules. He thought, for instance, that if he decided one morning that he wanted some dental work done, he should just phone a dentist's office and announce that he was coming.

That perspective was blueprint for a clash with the court system and its rigid rules. When he handed the will to the clerk of court's assistant, she examined it and said that we would have to get two of the witnesses to validate their signatures. Pop said, in no uncertain terms, that we couldn't do that — didn't even know whether the witnesses were dead or alive after all these years and wouldn't have a notion about where to start looking for them even if we were going to look for them, which we weren't.

He thought the woman's order was preposterous. She didn't bat an eye, just told us to come back when we had the witnesses. So Pop and I went sleuthing.

Amazingly, we found two of the witnesses living in Charlotte and still well enough for us to pick them up to go with us to the clerk's office. Pop never was convinced of the necessity of all that, but it became clear even to him that there were rules we were going to have to follow. With some muttering about "all this foolishness," we proceeded without another hitch and were through in seven months. As I worked this time, I began making notes for my children.

Not long from the time Mom's estate was closed, a professional colleague of my husband's was out jogging early one morning and, at age 52, drew his last breath and dropped to the pavement. I went to see his wife and offered help.

Her husband was a United Methodist minister, and that can leave a bereaved family with a uniquely difficult situation added to all the usual trauma. They lose their home, which is owned and furnished by the church. They must move out for a new minister to move in.

As I helped this widow gather information to take to her lawyer, I began to wonder if there was any way my mounting experience could be used to ease the enormous stress inevitable for other clergy spouses who face similar circumstances. I couldn't find them new homes and support systems or rear their children, but maybe I could clarify some of the estate settlement process.

I began expanding my notes. I developed a few pages and sent them to friends who were also interested in helping clergy spouses. Incorporating some of their comments and my answers to their questions, I then sent the result to 12 widows for their input.

After working with their ideas, I decided I'd better get a lawyer to go over what I had done. He made corrections and asked pointed questions. Trying to answer them brought me face-to-face with the inadequacy of my material. There were aspects of the process I hadn't explained clearly enough, others I hadn't even addressed. I returned to research and writing.

In January of 1991, Uncle Gene died. His will named his sister-in-law (my aunt) and me as coexecutrices of his estate. Because Gene had not been able to decide on specific bequests, he had his will drawn to distribute his estate equally between his siblings (as would have been the case if he had died intestate) and, if his siblings had died, to their heirs. The result was that this estate was now to be divided among all the living relatives of two generations.

I thought, "What now?"

The co-executrix was very willing to do her share, but by this time my husband and I had moved to Greensboro and she lived in Concord, not exactly next door. She felt that since I had been handling Uncle Gene's business affairs for several years, I was most familiar with what had to be done.

It made sense for me to assume major responsibility. I made an appointment with a lawyer who had known Uncle Gene and was somewhat familiar with his circumstances. I told him of the writing and research I was doing, showed him the estate inventory and the list of beneficiaries, and asked if he saw any reason for legal help.

He asked some questions, made a few suggestions and told me to come back if I encountered problems. He said he would even give me the checklist he used, and he gave me a copy from his file.

When I later looked over what he had given me, it reminded me of two matters I hadn't yet addressed in my manuscript — the right to elect a life estate and the significance of the tax clearance — but much more importantly, it helped me see a way to make my writing more usable. I needed to add a checklist. It would serve as a straight, clear path through what might seem an impregnable forest.

Even though I had already numbered steps and had provided lines for checking them off when completed, I saw that a list of the steps, placed at the beginning, would enable a whole view with the end in sight. That should keep a reader from experiencing the sense of bewilderment I had felt when I first began.

Back at the computer, I developed my checklist and tied my guidelines directly to it. I put copies of the manuscript into the hands of two CPAs and a lawyer for their corrections and suggestions.

When I finished incorporating their responses, I looked at what I had and knew it was now too bulky for copying and distributing to bereaved clergy spouses. I also realized that, except for an appendix about their benefits, the information wasn't geared toward their needs any more than anyone else's.

Wasn't the process the same whether the person

who died had been banker, ditch digger, teacher, factory worker, or artist? And what about all those who were helping parents, friends, aunts or uncles, as I had done, and who were experiencing frustration? It took a while for the questions to move me toward looking for the names of North Carolina publishers.

Pop died in December of 1991. His strong constitution had served him well. He had remarried not long before his 89th birthday and moved with his bride to The Methodist Home where the two of them had three good years. My husband was working on that estate as I neared the closing of Uncle Gene's.

During that time, while still deeply involved in my responsibilities as executrix and experiencing considerable stress related to them, I dreamed one night that I was very heavy with child. Labor pains were, in fact, beginning. I struggled up some stairs and made my way to what I knew was the birthing bed — a big, old four-poster.

I was mildly surprised to see Uncle Gene standing quietly at the head of the bed. He smiled but didn't speak. His presence seemed a comfort as I lay down and began to cooperate with the contractions.

When I awoke and thought about the dream, I felt it had to do with the estate settlement process I was in. I liked the image of Uncle Gene's support and encouragement. I also felt comfort in the image that something new was soon going to be born and I would feel better. I assumed that what was being birthed was the final estate accounting.

Perhaps, instead, the babe in the dream was the book in your hands.

Introduction

Harnessed to death and taxes comes another experience few escape: the settlement of an estate.

The odds have it that each of us will render, or help render, this service for at least one parent, other relative, friend, or mate. When faced with the job, however, most of us have no idea what to do, and we grope our way through months of confusion as we learn. During several experiences with estate settlement, I found no clear, step-by-step guidelines to help me perceive the process as a whole and understand how to negotiate the route to final accounting.

This book was written to fill the void I discovered. It is designed for those who have primary responsibility for the work of estate settlement, but relatives or friends who assist them may also find it helpful.

I have worked with care and diligence in my attempt to make this book both accurate and adequate. The small estates information, the checklist and guidelines were submitted to the scrutiny of two lawyers and two persons with experience in the office of the clerk of superior court. Appendix B was written in consultation with a third attorney, and my checklist draws from sharing by yet another. The tax information was reviewed by two certified public accountants. Corrections and suggestions by all of those professionals were incorporated into the text.

Nevertheless, this book is not intended to be, and should not be interpreted to be, advice on the law or legal procedures applicable to particular, individual estates or situations. I, the author, am not a lawyer and do not claim to be an authority on the interpretation of laws or on legal procedures.

This book does not cover all aspects of every estate or any particular estate, and I do not claim that it contains no errors. Laws are subject to repeal and amendment. The application of laws and legal procedures to any particular estate or individual situation requires consultation with competent professional advisors.

During the years I gathered the information in this book, my primary sources were: seven lawyers; seven clerks or their assistants; several accountants; innumerable employees of banks or other institutions, Vol. 7 of the *General Statutes of North Carolina* and other books (see Resources). In addition to the fact that laws can change, neither my sources nor I were infallible. No amount of research could guarantee a flawless text to cover every contingency.

Does this invalidate the usefulness of this book? I think not. If all of us waited to share information until we could assure infallibility, ours would be a silent species. We attempt to help each other as we share the best we can; and the more information we gather from persons who at least aim at the highest of standards, the more possibilities we discern, the more able we are to investigate, compare, question and learn — and the more likely we are to do a good job with the task at hand. Whether most of the estate settlement work is done by a lay person, a professional, or by the two working together, the process and product should benefit from the lay person's being as well-informed as possible.

I am a nonprofessional attempting to put my experience and research into language helpful to those who are faced with estate responsibilities.

It is my hope that this book will fulfill three goals:

1. Enable the person responsible for an estate settlement to work with a sense of direction and progress.

2. Aid communication with the clerk of superior court, with any lawyer or accountant who might be hired, with bank or investment institution employees and with those who benefit from the estate.

3. Provide an easy-to-use reference for much information applicable to most estate settlements — and point the direction for additional help.

Contents

Glossary

Administrator or administratrix: man or woman who is appointed by the clerk of superior Court to settle an estate when there is no will. (The words may be used to refer to others, but not in this text.)

Affiant: one who swears to an affidavit and is thereby given authority to do the work for an estate settlement, usually for a small estate.

Affidavit: a written statement made under oath before an authorized officer.

Beneficiary: one who benefits from something. ("Beneficiary" seems most often used to designate one who benefits from an estate by virtue of a will; "heir" is used for one whose entitlement to property is due under law if there is no will. This text sometimes uses "beneficiary" in its more general sense to mean one who receives property from any type estate.)

Bequeath: to leave something to someone through a will.

Bequest: that which is bequeathed.

1

Claim: 1. a right to something; 2. a written statement, meeting legal requirements, presented to the personal representative or clerk, which declares something due from the estate. ("Claim" is commonly used for a declaration of liability presented after the decedent's death and "debt" for a liability known before the death. Debts, however, also have a legal claim against the estate. Therefore, "claim" may encompass both.)

Clerk: clerk of superior court; should in each case be read to mean clerk or clerk's deputy or assistant.

Codicil: a legal document, made after the will, which modifies the will.

Debt: something owed. (Commonly used to mean a liability acknowledged before the decedent's death.)

Decedent: the one who died.

Devise: the act of giving or disposing of property by a will; property devised by will.

Devisee: one to whom a devise of property is made.

Dissent: not give assent to. (Dissenting from a will requires correct procedure by a deadline.)

Estate: everything of value belonging to the decedent or due the decedent — and the decedent's liabilities.

Executor or executrix: man or woman named in a will who qualifies before the clerk to carry out the will's directives.

Fiduciary: involving confidence or trust. A personal representative acts in a fiduciary capacity.

Formal administration: the process whereby the court oversees the administration of an estate through an appointed administrator or executor.

Heir: See note by "beneficiary."

Intestate: without having a valid will.

Inventory: list of property and property values.

Letter of Administration: the paper proving an administrator's authority.

Letter Testamentary: the paper proving an executor's authority.

Liens and encumbrances: usually legal claims (mortgages, etc.)

Lineal descendant: being in direct male or female line of ancestry; legally adopted children (and illegitimate children in regard to a female's estate) as well as bloodline legitimate children.

Non-probate asset: property not available for claims against the estate and not subject to distribution by the PR.

Personal property: everything other than real property; money, bank accounts, automobiles and other vehicles, boats, crops, IOU's, stocks, bonds, etc.

Personalty: personal property.

PR or personal representative: executor, executrix, administrator, administratrix.

Probate asset: property which is subject to claims against the estate and, after claims satisfaction, to distribution by the PR.

3

Probating a will: presenting a will to the clerk and having the clerk declare it to be genuine and officially on file.

Property: something of value belonging to a person; either "real property" or "personal property."

Qualification: the process whereby an application to administer an estate is approved by the clerk and the applicant takes oath as PR.

Real property: land and buildings.

Realty: real property.

Residuary: any part of the estate remaining after all debts and claims have been satisfied and specific bequests have been honored.

Tangible: capable of being perceived by touch.

Testate: having a valid will.

Chapter 1

The Job
and
Sources of Help

Whenever a person dies, he or she leaves an estate, and somebody must deal with it

Whether the estate is large or small and whether or not the decedent left a will, someone must gather information about what the decedent owned and owed, make a list of those entitled to property and give that information to the clerk of superior court. Someone must take responsibility for the estate, pay debts and taxes and pass along remaining property to beneficiaries. Except for the simplest of estates, the work is likely to require managing the decedent's property during the settlement process so that its value is protected for creditors and beneficiaries.

If you take an oath to do this job, you are accountable for the estate whether you do the work yourself or hire it done. Accountability demands accurate and complete records.

Time required for a simple settlement may be minimal; complex settlements sometimes stretch through several years. If an executor or administrator must qualify, the estate cannot be closed in less than three months. Whatever the time frame, there are a few deadlines which must be met.

Help available

A. Clerk: (In this text, the word "clerk" should always be read to mean the clerk of superior court or that clerk's deputy or assistant.) The clerk can be helpful in many ways, explaining some procedures and telling you about necessary accountings and when they are due to that office. The clerk is, however, forbidden to practice law and cannot do your work for you or deal with beneficiaries. (GS84-4)

B. Lawyer: if your work necessitates the drawing of legal contracts or if someone initiates legal action (to contest a will, for example), you will need to hire a lawyer to deal with those situations. If questions arise about legal rights and responsibilities, you will need legal advice. Even lacking those circumstances, it would be wise to have a lawyer review the inventory and beneficiary information (and will, if there is one) for any sizable or complex estate. He or she may spot some potential problem and be able to tell you how to avoid it. Or a lawyer may be aware of statutes or procedures that could benefit your situation. Such a review (preferably early in the process) may save the estate money in the long run; lack of it could, in some cases, prove costly.

You may also choose to hire a lawyer to handle any responsibilities you don't have time for or don't feel capable of handling — or even to do all the estate work except that which only you can do.

Whether you actually need a lawyer to do the

required routine tasks depends a great deal on your everyday skills, your time, and your emotional and physical health.

Is handling details something you do well? Can you keep good records, keep at a task, gather facts, meet deadlines? Are you up to the job? If you're grieving, work can be therapeutic, but you must sense your limits.

If you hire a lawyer, you should only hire one with certification to do probate work or one who at least has extensive experience and an excellent record with estates. Read Appendix B before hiring.

C. Certified public accountant: For completing and filing tax returns, you are likely to need to hire someone with special training and experience in that work. Some lawyers are qualified to do tax returns, including inheritance, estate, and fiduciary returns; some have staff members qualified to do them. Unless you hire such a lawyer, however, you will need to hire an accountant.

Before hiring either, do some comparison of fees and qualifications; just being a lawyer or accountant does not automatically make one competent to do estate returns. The person who does the returns should also be able to advise you about tax advantages in the timing of property distribution, payment of large debts and the like. Read Appendix B before hiring.

D. Funeral home: Some funeral homes will notify social security to stop benefit payments to the deceased so that payments won't have to be returned. Some will get death certificates for you. (Some also offer grief counseling, support groups, etc.)

E. This book: Read the introduction to see what this book is designed to do, and look over the table of contents to learn the scope of material available. Then, if the sole beneficiary is the spouse, or if you think the estate may be considered small, read Chapter 2. Otherwise, go to Chapters 3 and 4. In either case, follow the suggestions up through taking beneficiary and property information to the clerk.

After looking at that information, the clerk will be able to say whether you will complete your responsibilities by using one of the procedures in Chapter 2 or whether someone must take oath and fulfill responsibilities outlined in the more extensive Checklist and Guidelines.

Chapter 2 includes small estates' deadlines and fees current as of this writing. Chapter 6 contains deadlines and fees common to the formal administration procedures outlined in Chapters 3 and 4.

There are, of course, some major differences in circumstances according to whether a decedent died testate (leaving a will) or intestate (without a will). When there are significant differences, a guideline will have separate information or suggestions designated by the words *testate* and *intestate*.

The checklist is an index to the guidelines and provides spaces for recording deadlines and checking off work you've completed. The checklist and guidelines are not intended to indicate a rigid order in which work must be done, nor will one guideline's tasks necessarily be completed before another is begun. Some order for tasks is, however, dictated by deadlines.

Soon after your qualification, locate the "Deadlines, Fees" section of the book. Use the information there to figure your projected deadlines and pencil them into the appropriate checklist blanks, but verify them with an authority before using those dates.

Throughout the book, the letters GS followed by numbers refer to General Statutes applicable to the subject discussed. This does not mean that those laws have been fully explained or interpreted, nor does it mean no other laws apply. This is simply a guide so that you may easily find those laws if you wish to read them.

It is important to know that local custom may affect the way an estate is handled. If you ask 10 clerks and lawyers in 10 counties to explain a 90-Day Inventory, for example, you're likely to discover differences. When approaching any professional with information gained from this book or elsewhere, a wise approach would be to say, "It is my understanding that.... Is this correct?"

You are now ready to take your first step toward completion of your responsibilities.

Chapter 2

Summary Administration; Small Estates Administration

Procedures for transfer of property without necessity of an executor or administrator

Under certain circumstances, an estate's property can be passed on to beneficiaries or creditors by means that are simpler than those dictated by a formal administration that requires an executor or administrator. Some of those circumstances and simpler means are discussed in this section.

Summary Administration
(GS28A-28)

Whether the decedent died testate, intestate, or partially testate, if the spouse is the sole devisee under the will and/or sole heir of intestate property, if no application or petition has been filed for appointment of a PR, if the devise to the spouse is not in trust, and if a will does not so prohibit, the spouse may file with the clerk a petition for an order of Summary Administration.

A property inventory, the will (if there is one), and other information required on the petition must be presented to the clerk. If the clerk determines that the spouse is entitled to summary administration, the clerk will enter an order to the effect that no other administration of the estate is necessary. The result is that the spouse assumes, to the extent of the value of property received, all remaining liabilities of the decedent, including taxes and valid claims against the decedent or estate, and uses certified copies of the petition to access property, etc.

This procedure should not be used, however, if a sale of real property is, or may become, necessary or desirable. In that case, a formal administration, with notice to creditors, will be necessary to assure that creditors will not have future rights.

Small Estates

The following procedures are designed for use with small estates. It seems feasible, however, that in rare circumstances they could also be used for a portion of the property of a more well-to-do decedent who had no real property to be endangered by lack of notice to creditors and whose personal property basically passed to beneficiaries as non-probate assets not needed to pay claims.

The clerk can tell you whether one or more of these methods can be used in the settlement with which you are concerned. An attorney also can tell you. What is written here will help you understand options that may be available. It should also help you know what questions to ask.

Settlement by the clerk
(Also called "Payment to the Clerk")

(GS28A-25-6)

If no personal representative has been appointed and if the total value which would have to be collected and disbursed in order to complete a settlement does not exceed the amount set by law, the clerk may be able to personally receive what is due the estate, pay the bills and distribute anything that remains. (At this writing, the maximum total amount that can be received by the clerk is $5,000.) This procedure is simple and usually takes little time. In one clerk's office I was told this method is often used for estates of persons whose resources have dwindled due to necessity of nursing home care or others with small resources and perhaps only a funeral bill to pay.

In every case, if there is a will, it must be taken to the clerk's office. Also take an inventory of what the decedent owned, what he or she owed and the names of those who should get any of the decedent's property that remains after bills are paid.

If there is a surviving spouse, the clerk can pay the spouse an allowance (at this writing, $10,000) from the estate's property before any debts are paid. In an estate which can be handled by the clerk, payment of part of a spouse's allowance will close the estate. In some cases, a motor vehicle instead of cash may be transferred as all or part of a spouse's allowance.

Eligible children or other dependents may also qualify for an allowance ($2,000 at this writing) that can be paid before debts are considered.

If not depleted by allowances, property will be used to pay creditors or will go to beneficiaries or heirs.

Settlement by affidavit
(GS28A-25-1 - GS28A-25-5)

What does "Settlement by Affidavit" mean?

It means that the person who will gather the property, pay debts and distribute remaining property will do so by authority shown by an affidavit. This person may be referred to as an affiant.

What estates may be settled by affidavit?

If no one has been appointed and no one has applied to be executor or administrator of the estate, and if the value of the decedent's personal property, less liens and encumbrances, is not greater than the amount allowed by law, the estate probably can be settled by affidavit.

At the time of this writing, if the sole heir or sole beneficiary of all the property is a surviving spouse not otherwise disqualified, the total personal property collectible by affidavit may exceed $10,000 but may not exceed $20,000 (GS28A-25-1). Other estates can qualify for this procedure if the value of the personal property is not more than $10,000; there can be real property over and above this limit. (If there is real property, ask an authority whether the affidavit process will clear the title sufficiently to do away with creditors' rights to proceeds if the property were to be sold within a few years.)

Who can take responsibility for the estate work?

If there is a will, the clerk can consider the named executor, a beneficiary, a creditor. If there is no will, an heir or creditor can be named.

If there is a will, what must be done with it?

It must be taken to the clerk of court. This can be done at any time before or on the same day the affidavit is filed (No.4 below). The person presenting the will will be given a copy.

What must be done to get the process started?

Whether or not there is a will, you (or a person willing and likely to be approved for doing the estate work) should:

1. Make a list of heirs or beneficiaries, giving addresses and relationship of each to the decedent.

2. Make a list of the decedent's bank or other accounts, vehicles, other property, and give the location and value for each. If you can't get the exact value, give an estimate. If you put land or a building on your list but don't have the deed, write down any information that will help identify the property. If you have the deed, take it with you to the clerk's office.

3. Wait at least the number of days set by law (at this writing, 30 days after the decedent died), then go to the clerk of superior court's office, estates division, at the courthouse. Take the following: name, date of death and place of death of the decedent, his or her social security number, the lists of beneficiaries and property.

4. Show the information you have brought. If you are approved for doing the work, a "qualifying" affidavit will be prepared, signed and filed. The clerk will

send a copy of the affidavit to each heir or beneficiary and will give you certified copies to use for your responsibilities.

What must the affiant do?

1. Present a copy of the affidavit wherever you need to gain access to the decedent's property. It gives you authority to do whatever must be done with bank accounts, share certificates, stocks, bonds, vehicle titles and other property so that you can pay bills and distribute what remains.

2. Pay everything that must be paid, but know that:

(a) A surviving spouse can receive an allowance ($10,000 at this writing) before any bills are paid. Children or other dependents may be eligible for an allowance that can be paid before bills are considered (child's allowance presently $2,000). Ask the clerk what you must do before allowances are paid.

(b) Costs of administration also are paid before creditors. At this writing they include a $36 qualifying fee, a fee of 40 cents per $100 of personal property value (minimum of $10), any lawyer's fee, etc.

(c) If there is not then enough property to pay all debts and claims, payment must be in a specific order. Ask an authority. You may also want to read "Consider Claims Priorities" (Guideline 5). (There may well be no taxes, but you are responsible for any due for the decedent, for the year before the year of death as well as for year of death, and any due for the estate.) If someone has paid bills that were correctly due from the estate, reimburse that person from estate funds.

3. Distribute any remaining property to heirs or

15

beneficiaries. If there was no will, property must be distributed according to laws that govern such distribution; those who may receive property are listed on a chart in Chapter 5. If there is a will, property is distributed according to its terms.

4. Go to the clerk of court and give the information needed for another affidavit. This one must show that you have collected the personal property and the manner in which you have distributed it. You must file this affidavit by its deadline (at this writing, 90 days after the filing of the qualifying affidavit) unless you show good reason for not being able to do so and are granted an extension.

At any time during this process, the affiant or any other person may apply to be appointed as personal representative to complete the estate work. (If, for example, real property should have to be sold to pay debts, an executor or administrator must be appointed by the clerk before that sale is possible.) If a personal representative is appointed, the affiant must turn responsibilities over to the PR and make complete accountings to the PR and clerk.

Transfer of motor vehicle
(GS20-77(b))
By form (presently No. 317)
from N.C. Department of Motor Vehicles

If no executor or administrator has qualified and no PR is, in the clerk's opinion, required to qualify, and if the clerk has not allotted the vehicle as part of a spouse allowance, the clerk and all of the estate's beneficiaries or heirs may use this form to transfer a vehicle title. There are affidavits on the form (not to be confused with the affidavits discussed above) to be signed by beneficiaries and a statement to be signed by the clerk.

With their signatures, beneficiaries agree on who gets the vehicle, and they state that the decedent's debts have been paid or that proceeds from the sale of the vehicle will be used to apply against those debts. In other words, they assume responsibility for those estate debts. This type vehicle transfer can be an effective tool in closing some estates.

If you need more help

If you need more help than the clerk is able to give, or if you have legal questions such as what someone's rights or responsibilities are, consult a lawyer. If you need to talk only briefly to a lawyer, you may call the N.C. Bar Association Lawyer Referral Service (1-800-662-7660) and request the name of a lawyer with whom you may talk for 30 minutes for a modest fee ($30 at this writing). If you need more help, read Appendix B and then hire the assistance you need.

17

Chapter 3

Checklist of Responsibilities*

Numbers match appropriate guidelines in Chapter 4. The few lines on the right are for noting deadlines.

_____ 1. Assess your circumstances; make a list of beneficiaries or heirs

_____ 2. Prepare preliminary inventory

_____ 3. Go to clerk of superior court's office:
• Apply for Letters (includes filing inventory and list of beneficiaries)
• take oath
• post bond if not waived
• get Letters
• ask questions

_____ 4. Get copies of death certificate

_____ 5. Notify creditors   _____
a. Publish notice
b. Mail or take notice to known creditors

_____ 6. Consider Claims Priorities

_____ 7. Order tax ID number (EIN),
      if necessary

_____ 8. Collect all assets/papers
      not collected for No. 2

_____ 9. Communicate with
      beneficiaries or heirs
      intestate only: notify
      spouse of right to life
      estate; get waiver if denied   _____

_____ 10. Apply for and pay spouse
      and/or children's allowances,
      if appropriate and desired   _____

_____ 11. Do any of the following which
      apply:

_____   a. Access/update existing
      accounts

_____   b. Open estate checking account

_____   c. Collect all debts

_____   d. Collect all insurance

_____   e. Look for and apply for
      other benefits

_____   f. Transact business related
      to real property

_____   g. Transact remaining
      personal property business

_____ 12. File 90-Day Inventory
      with clerk of court   _____

_____ 13. Send notice of
      fiduciary relationship

_____ 14. File decedent's state and
      federal income tax returns,
      prior year, if not already filed   _____

_____ 15. Pay debts and claims

_____ 16. File decedent's final state
and federal income tax returns   _____

_____ 17. File N.C. estate tax return
OR tax certification   _____

_____ 18. File federal estate tax return,
if necessary   _____

_____ 19. Receive tax clearance,
if applicable

_____ 20. File fiduciary tax returns,
if necessary   _____

_____ 21. File annual account with
clerk of court, if necessary   _____

_____ 22. Determine net shares due
beneficiaries or heirs

_____ 23. Complete distribution
of estate; get receipts

_____ 24. File final account
with clerk of court   _____

_____ 25. Notify IRS of
termination of responsibility

*For my checklist, I have drawn heavily from an intraoffice checklist given to me by Archie Smith, Jr., an attorney with the firm of Smith, Casper, Smith, and Alexander in Asheboro, North Carolina.

Chapter 4

Guidelines
for
Settling an Estate
(With or Without a Will)

To use these guidelines with ease and skill, it is essential that you first read Chapter 1.

Words enclosed in brackets indicate a figure that can be found in Chapter 6.

1. Assess your circumstances and make a list of beneficiaries or heirs.

Testate: Your goal is to distribute the decedent's property according to the terms of the will. A copy of the will may be used as your reference, but the original must be presented to the clerk of court for probate. If the original is not found in the home, check to see if it might be in a bank lockbox, with the attorney who prepared it, or on file at the clerk's office. A thorough search should also be made for subsequent wills or codicils.

When satisfied that you have the needed documents, examine them. There may be factors to consider that are not mentioned below (verification of handwriting of a handwritten will, for example). If so, the clerk or a lawyer can guide you.

Note whether signatures of witnesses were notarized and an affidavit attached. If not, the clerk may require that you locate two of the witnesses and have them verify their signatures.

Note what is said, if anything, about necessity of bond.

Make a list of beneficiaries. If any beneficiaries have died since the will was written, include their names, indicating that they are deceased. (S.L. 199-45 specifies who may receive in place of a deceased devisee.) You will need beneficiaries' ages — at least whether they are adults or children — and addresses. (You may later need their social security numbers. If you must check on ages or addresses, it may save a step to get social security numbers at the same time.) In some situations, a trust named in the will may be listed as a beneficiary. Unless you learn that the estate can be settled by Small Estates procedures or Summary Administration, the list will go on your Application for Probate and Letters. See Guideline 3.

Note what is left to a surviving spouse. Statutes allow some grounds for dissent. Currently, if what passes to the surviving spouse outside the will (life insurance proceeds, etc.) plus what is left to the spouse through the will is not greater than what he or she would have received if there had been no will, the spouse has the right to dissent and take the intestate share. There is a [deadline] and required procedure. (Spouse rights: GS30 and 31A) A pending bill proposes revisions of options and procedures.

If applicable, add onto your checklist a line for this deadline.

If the decedent was divorced, married, had (or adopted) children after the will was written, or if renouncing a bequest might actually have some tax or other advantage for a beneficiary, or if any other rights questions arise, talk with a lawyer. There is a renunciation deadline. (Renunciation: GS31B)

If a trust is established by the will, the wording will determine how the trust must be handled and whether the trustee has to "qualify" for that responsibility, one not necessarily covered by the executor's qualification.

Though Guideline 3 mentions presentation of the will for probate at the same time as qualification, the will may be given to the clerk before that time. If, however, a named executor does not plan to qualify soon after the will has been probated, timing should be discussed with the clerk.

Intestate: When a person dies without leaving a will to guide the court in overseeing administration of the estate, his or her property must be distributed according to state laws that were written with the intent of protecting the decedent's heirs. The heirs and their shares of the estate are determined by law.

Make a list of heirs. You will need their ages and addresses. (If you must check on ages or addresses, it may save a step to get their social security numbers at the same time. Those numbers may later be required for tax returns.)

The following are possibilities for your list of heirs: surviving spouse, surviving children, lineal descendants of deceased children, the decedent's parents if the decedent had no children or other lineal descendants. If any of the above have died since the decedent's death, note that beside the name. Other possible heirs are listed on the chart in Chapter 5. The chart will also give you an idea of what will be involved in distributing the estate. (Unless the clerk determines that the estate can be settled by a Chapter 2 procedure, the list of heirs will go on the Application for Letters of Administration. See Guideline 3.)

An heir or creditor may apply to administer the estate. The order of preference for appointment is: surviving spouse, an heir other than the spouse, a creditor to whom the decedent owed something at the time of death, any person of good character unless disqualified. Any of these may, with good cause, waive the right to serve and ask that someone else be appointed.

Executors and administrators for both *testate* and *intestate* estates are correctly referred to as personal representatives or PR's. For personal representatives' powers, duties and liabilities, see GS28A-13-1 through GS28A-13-13.

2. Prepare preliminary estate inventory, one copy for yourself and one for the clerk of superior court.

Unless you can use Small Estates procedures or Summary Administration, an inventory of all the decedent's assets, along with the approximate value of each, will need to be copied onto, or attached to, an application for appointment as PR. The application form is available from the clerk's office. Getting it and its sheet of instructions ahead of time will enable you to complete it more accurately, but remember that it and all other probate forms must be signed in the presence of the clerk, or signatures must be notarized.

Testate: Use the Application for Probate and Letters.

Intestate: Use the Application for Letters of Administration.

Testate and Intestate: You may not be able to develop a complete estate inventory before submitting your Application to the clerk. That is acceptable. Omissions at this point won't create any real problems though they may cause some inconvenience in that, based on the listing, the clerk will give you the number of Letters (see Guideline 3) needed for accessing property. You can, of course, get additional Letters at a later time.

If there is a lockbox wholly or partially in the decedent's name, it must be inventoried by a qualified person before any of its contents can be legally removed. A qualified person is one named as lessee or co-tenant of the safe-deposit box or one possessing a letter of administration, letter testamentary, affidavit of collection, an order of summary administration or other letter signed by the clerk of court. If a person so qualified is not available, then the presence of the clerk of superior court of the county where the box is located, or of the clerk's representative, is required.

A copy of the inventory is to be furnished to the institution where the box is located, and a copy is to be given to the person possessing a key to the lockbox if that person is someone other than the qualified person.

If the box contains any writing that appears to be a will, codicil or any other instrument of a testamentary nature, the qualified person or the clerk must then file it in the office of the clerk of superior court. Other contents of the box may not be released by the institution to anyone other than a qualified person (GS28A-15-13).

The qualified person should be sure to take the lockbox key when going to make the inventory; if it can't be found, the box will have to be drilled open [at considerable cost].

If there are no good records of additional property, you may be able to construct a fairly complete listing by reviewing income tax returns, canceled checks, property insurance and statements from banks and brokers. Guideline 8 mentions some other significant papers you may find. Register of Deeds and county tax offices can provide real property information if needed.

Because of buy-outs, mergers, name changes, etc., finding the name of the company that's accountable for a stock certificate or insurance policy may require some perseverance.

The application asks for both personal and real property and their values. If accurate values are not yet available, probable values are acceptable on this preliminary inventory. Try not to overestimate or you could later have to explain to the court or to tax authorities what happened to value that never really existed.

The inventory section of the application is designed to divide the estate into three categories: (a) those assets readily available to the PR for payments to creditors and for distribution to beneficiaries; (b) those assets not ordinarily available to the PR but which can perhaps, under some circumstances, be legally accessed and used to pay debts; (c) property not generally accessible, recoverable, for claims but which may also be considered when determining the taxable estate. (The value of the taxable estate may be *very* different from that of the property available to the PR.) The listing is also for beneficiaries' information.

Sometimes all of an asset's value is available to the PR for satisfying creditors or for distribution to beneficiaries, and sometimes only a portion of its value is available. If, for example, the only name on a bank account is that of the decedent, the total value of the account is available to the PR (i.e. is probate property). If, however, the asset is jointly owned, only the decedent's share of it can be considered as potential probate property.

Whether the decedent's share of a jointly owned asset actually IS probate property is determined, at this point, by whether the contract (often a signature card) indicates a right-of-survivorship agreement. If the asset was jointly owned by the decedent and one other person and was owned *without* right of survivorship, 50 percent of the value will definitely be available for creditors or beneficiaries. If ownership was by the decedent and two other persons *without* right of survivorship, 33 1/3 percent of the value is probate property, etc. You will need to clearly indicate both the total balance and the decedent's share (percentage).

If the contract indicates right of survivorship, the decedent's share is not, and cannot become, probate property unless other assets are not sufficient to meet creditors' claims — and even then, only in certain circumstances. If some right-of-survivorship property must be used to satisfy claims, read "Joint Accounts" in the "Account Options" chapter of this book and also ask the clerk or an attorney to guide you. The decedent's share from an account with right of survivorship under GS41, for instance, is more readily accessible for claims than one from an account established under GS53-146.

The instructions indicate that a lump sum for the value of the property in some categories is acceptable for this inventory. For household furnishings, a nominal lump-sum value is usually acceptable here. If the family agrees on distribution of those furnishings, it is likely that the same figure will be acceptable for the 90-Day Inventory. Family disputes may result in necessity of appraisals.

When estimating the value of real property, don't forget to subtract mortgages, taxes due, or other legal claims against it. Unless real property must be sold to pay debts and claims, or unless a will's wording makes it so, it is not part of the probate estate.

(For more on inventories and accountings, see GSA28A-20-1 through 28A-21-5.)

The instructions clarify "Other Personal Property Recoverable under GS28A-15-10," "Transfers Over Which Decedent Retained Any Interest Described in ...(GS105-3(3)..." and "Claim For Wrongful Death," and mention consultation with an attorney if you believe any of these apply to the estate with which you are working. These are among the possibilities that can require work beyond the normal scope of the job of administration.

If you discover that estate property may be being held by someone who is not disclosing it, there is a process that the clerk can initiate to require that person to appear before the clerk for questioning (GS28A-15-12)

If your inventory is too long for space provided, construct all or part of it separately, and write "see attached list" on the form. (Use the application's format.) Copy totals onto the form.

Before giving your application to the clerk, you may want to go by or call to ask some questions. Asking "When is the best time to come?" may help you avoid a long wait. Other questions might include:

Testate: If there is no affidavit and notary seal on the will, ask, "Must I have witnesses' signatures verified? If so, what is the procedure?" If the will's named executor cannot or does not wish to serve and you want to serve instead, or if you are the named executor and you live out of state, ask the clerk what procedure is required. If the will doesn't specifically waive bond, ask, "Must bond be posted and, if so, how much?" (Bond is rarely required unless the will specifies it, but is sometimes required for out-of-state executors.)

Intestate: Ask if you must post bond and, if so, how much it will be and how to go about it. If you live in North Carolina and if all heirs are over 18 years old and all sign permission for bond to be waived, or if you are the estate's sole heir, no bond will be required. Under other circumstances, a bond may be required. (GS28A-8-1)

You may save yourself considerable time if you stay aware, now, of requirements for your next accounting to the clerk — the "Inventory (AOC E-505)" referred to on the application. This is the accounting often called the "90-Day Inventory" because it must be made within three months of qualification. If you know what you're going to need, you can perhaps ask some of the right questions, get needed papers and make accurate notes as you gather information for the preliminary inventory.

For the 90-Day Inventory (Guideline 12), estimations will not be acceptable. You will be expected to give an accurate and complete itemized accounting of property, with *exact date-of-death* values that include, when applicable, interest or dividends accrued to the date of death.

For real property try to get the address, acreage, deed book and page number as well as names on the deeds.

As indicated in the instructions for the Application, the clerk will want to see signature cards or deposit contracts for all joint bank accounts. Financial institutions can provide duplicates of original contracts.

And though the clerk isn't likely to require seeing them, be aware, as you go through papers, that only the contracts for insurance, annuities, IRAs, trusts, stocks/bonds, etc., can clarify, with certainty, whether the asset is transferred directly to one or more beneficiaries or whether some/all of the value goes to the estate and becomes probate property.

Also be aware (though not specifically for the 90-Day Inventory) that you will soon need to know what papers each bank and other institution will require in order for you to access accounts; so if you're asking them other questions now, add that one.

It will be important, by the time you submit the 90-Day Inventory, for you to know the difference between probate and non-probate assets. Court fees will be charged on the value of probate assets, and though corrections can be made on the annual or final account, avoiding mistakes or omissions saves time.

3. Go to the estates division of the clerk's office in the courthouse in the county in which the decedent lived — or if non-resident, in county where property was held. You may want to have someone with you to help listen and ask questions.

Take the list of beneficiaries and preliminary inventory you prepared, the decedent's address, date of death and social security number, and the will if there is one. If the clerk looks at your inventory and says you do not have to qualify as personal representative, you will be directed to use procedures outlined in Chapter 2. Otherwise, you will complete your application for appointment as PR and continue with these guidelines. (Appointment of PR: GS28A-6-1 through 7-1) If two persons consider being co-PRs and have the option, they should consider the advantages of wording that allows either of them, rather than requiring both of them, to sign checks and other documents.

Testate: Give the clerk the will and your completed Application for Probate and Letters. (After taking oath, you will be given Letters Testamentary.)

Intestate: Give the clerk your completed Application for Administration. (After taking oath, you will be given Letters of Administration.)

Testate and Intestate: Post bond if not waived, take oath, and get the Letters appropriate for your situation. These Letters validate your authority to do your work. The date on which the Letters are granted is the "date of qualification," and you will notice that several checklist deadlines come a certain period "after qualification." There is a qualification [fee].

On the basis of your inventory, the clerk will suggest the number of Letters you will need. You will, at the least, need one for each financial institution where there are probate assets and one for each vehicle to be transferred. (You may not want to get Letters for stocks or bonds without asking an agent whether Letters dated closer to the transfer will be required.) The IRS requires a Letter with your notice of fiduciary relationship. Clerks aren't responsible for tax returns and may not think to remind you of this. You may get five Letters free. Additional copies require a small [fee].

While at the clerk's office, be sure to get AOC's most current "Estates Procedures Pamphlet." Look at its instructions for notice to creditors (my Guideline 5) and ask any questions you may have. Also ask how many death certificates you are likely to need. Ask whether the clerk sends notices to heirs or beneficiaries or if you are responsible for doing so. Ask whether the clerk provides the receipts which you must get beneficiaries or heirs to sign for all property transferred to them. If you are responsible for preparing and wording the receipts, ask about wording. Get the form needed for your next accounting to the clerk (Inventory, AOC E-505) and confirm the due date.

4. Get copies of the death certificate.

Death certificates, required by most banks, insurance companies, etc., are available from the Register of Deeds or, in some counties, from the County Health Department. If you prefer, the funeral home may get them for you. Carefully check certificates for accuracy of information and spelling. Each certificate costs [a few dollars.]

5. Notify creditors.

a. Publish the notice to creditors (wording as instructed by the clerk) as soon as possible after qualification. It must state a [deadline] by which creditors must present claims. The notice must be published once a week for four consecutive weeks in a newspaper qualified to publish such legal advertisements for the county. (If no such newspaper is published in the county, the clerk will tell you what you must do.) Check accuracy of first published notice and see that any necessary corrections are made immediately. After last publication, an affidavit of publication from the newspaper's accounting office must be filed with the clerk.

b. Mail the notice to creditors [within a certain period after qualification]. You must mail, first class, or hand deliver, the notice to any creditor who may have a rightful claim. You are required to make a serious effort to discover all creditors. Checking with family members, searching decedent's papers, etc., would indicate serious effort. If you feel you should get proof that the notice was received, send it by certified mail. The clerk may require, at the same time the publication affidavit is required, an affidavit that a notice was mailed to each creditor entitled to it. I understand the law GS28A-14-1 to say that the notice does not have to be mailed to those creditors whose claims you already recognize as valid and which you are committed to paying.

6. Consider claims priorities.

VERY IMPORTANT: SOME CLAIMS HAVE LEGAL PRIORITY OVER OTHERS AND YOU CAN BE HELD PERSONALLY LIABLE IF YOU EXHAUST THE ESTATE'S RESOURCES BY PAYING LOWER-PRIORITY CLAIMS AND THEN RECEIVE A HIGHER-PRIORITY CLAIM BEFORE THE DEADLINE.

Because of the possibility of unanticipated claims, do not pay anything until the deadline has passed. Then, if the estate is not large enough to cover all liabilities, claims must be grouped and arranged according to priorities set by law. They must then be paid according to those priorities and payment may have to be prorated, meaning that some claims may have to be only partially satisfied. If estate liabilities are considerably greater than the estate assets, some creditors might not be paid at all, and beneficiaries may not receive anything.

An allowance may be paid to a surviving spouse and to eligible children and other dependents before any creditors are considered (Guideline 10).

Costs of administration (payments to clerk of court, attorney's fee, PR's fee, fee for notice publication, perhaps bond premium, etc.) are also paid before the seven classes listed below.

As personal representative, you may receive a fee of up to 5 percent of receipts and disbursements (except a few, such as a lawyer's fee). (GS28A-23-3) When determining potential fee, value of real property is not considered unless the will orders it sold (in which case the entire amount is considered) or unless it must be sold to pay debts (in which case the portion used for debts can be considered). The fee is determined by the clerk. Within limits set by the above, the clerk will consider time, responsibility, liability, trouble and skill required of you. In some counties, the PR files a petition for a fee; in others, the clerk sets the fee without such a petition. If you do not want a fee, make that clear. PR's fees must be reported as income on tax returns. If you are the estate's sole beneficiary, you will not want to receive a fee since the money will be coming to you otherwise without taxes due.

After payment of allowances for spouse and children and payment of administration costs, if there is not enough property to totally satisfy all debts and claims, they must be grouped in classes and paid according to the claims-priority order below (GS28-19-6). Ask an authority to guide you; the listing may help you understand.

(1) Legal claims that have a specific lien on property — to an amount not greater than the property's value.

(2) Funeral expenses [to a specified limit, which does not include cemetery lot and gravestone].

(3) All taxes, dues (such as interest, penalties), and other claims (anything that might be due the U.S. gov-

ernment) that have preference according to United States law.

(4) All taxes, dues (such as interest, penalties), and other claims that have preference under the laws of the State of N.C. and its subdivisions (local governments).

(5) Judgments, docketed and in force, made by any courts of competent jurisdiction within North Carolina — to the extent that they are a lien on the decedent's property at the time of death.

(6) Wages due anyone employed by the decedent, those claims for wages going back no further than 12 months immediately before the death; or if the employee was employed for the year in which the decedent died, then from the time of such employment. Medical services, supplies, drugs necessary to treat the decedent during final illness (the period of such illness not to be counted as lasting longer than the 12 months before the death).

(7) All other cases.

Most evidences of estate liabilities are simply unsurprising bills you have no reason to question. The decedent, however, may have asked cousin Bob to paint rental property in Ohio and Bob, not knowing of the death, did the painting after the decedent died. Or three years ago the decedent may have made an oral agreement with Lyn Doe for a four-year loan. In such cases, Bob and Lyn may present unexpected claims against the estate.

Claims should be written, contain required information, and be personally delivered or mailed to you or the clerk or sent by registered or certified mail. If you doubt whether a claim should be paid, check with the clerk or an attorney.

There are procedures to follow for requiring further evidence or for rejecting claims. (GS28A-19-2 and 19-16).

If someone wants to take responsibility for a claim and relieve the estate of it, there is a process for doing that. (GS28A-19-7) If property would have to be sold to meet debts, for example, some family members might want to personally assume the debts in order to keep the property from being sold.

With very few exceptions, if a claim is presented after the date specified in the notice to creditors and it is for debts incurred before the decedent's death, the claim does not have to be satisfied. Check with an authority, however, before denying one. Some claims that arise at or after the death have additional time in which they can be presented (GS28A-19-3).

At any time after the deadline in the notice to the creditors, you may provide evidence to the clerk that all debts and claims have been satisfied, present the final account to be reviewed and audited, and upon the accounting's approval, be discharged from your duties.

Beneficiaries' and heirs' rights to property are considered only after allowances, costs of administration and the 7 classes of debts and claims — so don't distribute any property until you are absolutely sure that none of its value will be needed to meet those obligations.

7. Order the taxpayer identification number (Employer Identification Number — EIN) for the

estate.

After the decedent's death, when a financial institution reports income to IRS it should be reported under the estate's identification number, the EIN, rather than under the decedent's social security number. The EIN is required for opening interest-bearing estate accounts, including a checking account, and it is required for filing federal tax returns for the estate. (You are liable for a [penalty] if the EIN is omitted from those returns).

To get the EIN, you need Form SS-4 from the IRS. You can order it by calling 1-800-829-3676, or you may be able to get it from your accountant or a local IRS office. If you want the EIN in less than 4 weeks, you will also need to get a set of instructions called "Request Your Employer Identification Number by Phone Instructions." If you get the EIN by phone, you still must mail the completed SS-4 as soon as possible. See Appendix D for other IRS forms you may need later and can get now.

8. Collect any of the decedent's assets and papers you haven't already pulled together.

Look for documents that indicate assets owned by or due to the decedent, debts owed by the decedent, other information you may need. These include tax returns, bank statements and signature cards, certificates of deposit, insurance policies, stock and bond certificates, IRA agreements, trust agreements, annuity contracts, social security number, credit cards, credit-card-company agreements which might reveal insurance on life or debts, mortgage agreements, loan agreements, business agreements, car registration and title, deeds, recent property appraisals, lease agreements, W-2 form from employer for last-year-of-life (in some cases a 1099 is issued in lieu of W-2), retirement plan agreements, booklets on employment benefits, membership benefit statements for clubs, union or other employee organizations to which the decedent belonged, military service papers, etc.

If the decedent had loaned property — vehicles, precious jewelry, collections, etc. — locate it and be sure you have access to it.

According to the benefits you may need to apply for, you may also have to have marriage certificate, adoption papers, birth certificates of spouse or children, divorce papers, prenuptial agreement, citizenship papers.

Intestate: If anyone ordered by the clerk to account for any property received from the decedent refuses to share, to the best of his or her knowledge, information about that property or about how he or she came to have that property, check with an authority to see if that person is to be considered to have already received his or her full share of the estate.

9. Notify beneficiaries and establish good communication.

Some clerks send notices to beneficiaries, some do not. Even if the clerk does, notification from you is a good idea. It should include: date of the death, date of your appointment, the fact that the person will benefit from the estate. (If there is a will, you may want to enclose a copy of the will or of that part in which the person is named.) You may explain what, if anything, is known at this point about when property might be transferred, but be careful not to say you will do something which you don't yet know that you can do.

You must not distribute any property until it has been determined for certain that the property won't be needed to meet obligations outlined in Guideline 6, nor until you have received tax clearance and made any necessary title changes. If a bequest is a percentage of the estate, its distribution cannot be completed until you are ready for final accounting.

You should always take into account the needs and concerns of beneficiaries. Whenever possible, major decisions should be made in consultation with them and with their approval. If there must be a sale, be certain they are notified, in person or by registered or certified mail, of the date and place so they have the opportunity of purchase. If there is any question about conflict of interest, get approval from the clerk before selling even personal property.

Intestate: A surviving spouse must be notified of the right to elect a life estate. If that right is denied, the spouse's waiver must be obtained. The option of electing a life estate is briefly explained at the end of Chapter 5. Electing the option or denying it must be done with the clerk, and there is a [deadline] by which it must be done.

10. Apply for allowances for spouse and children, if applicable and desired.

Check to see if the spouse wants the allowance. If so, check with the clerk concerning procedure and see that application is made within the [deadline]. This allowance, the [limit of which is set by law], is available for the first year after the death and can be paid before creditors are considered. (GS30-15)

If the deceased was survived by eligible children or other dependents, they may also [receive an allowance] which can be paid before creditors are considered. Check eligibility with the clerk. You are responsible for checking and following required procedure. (GS30-17)

Testate: It is my understanding of the law that if the allowance to the spouse is paid, that amount will then be deducted from any bequest made in the will.

11. Do any of the following which apply to the assets and liabilities in your care.

Work in this category, especially, cannot be neatly packaged to follow the preceding step, nor will it have been completed before the next. Reminders are simply grouped here to assist a more complete overview.

A. Access and update existing accounts.

Promptly contact each financial institution where the decedent had accounts. Give notification of date of death and date of your appointment. Give any account-identifying information you have such as account numbers and names on accounts. Ask whether there may be accounts you do not know about which bear the decedent's name. Ask what you must provide to access the accounts: Letter Testamentary or Letter of Administration? Death certificate? Anything else? Ask if they have any other instructions for you.

As soon as you give the bank or other institution

the Letter authorizing your appointment, you have legal responsibility for handling the funds in those accounts as wisely as possible for the protection and benefit of creditors and beneficiaries. Though an institution's employees will, when asked, try to explain their policies and your options, you should ask enough questions and be sure you understand answers well enough to avoid losing money due to unnecessary penalties or oversight. Funds which may possibly be used to pay debts and claims should be kept identifiable and reasonably accessible until all such liabilities are satisfied. For more specific information about account options available to you, read Appendix C.

Get the following figures that will be needed for 90-Day Inventory and/or tax returns:

A "date of death" balance for each account.

• A separate interest figure for any interest accrued but not posted at the date of death, which would have been payable on the date of death. This figure may not be available for every account.

• Total interest earned on the account from January 1, year of death, to the date of death.

Ask about length of time required for transferring funds into a beneficiary's name or for closing the account and receiving the check. If stocks and bonds are involved, the process can take considerable time. U.S. government bonds may need to be submitted six or more weeks before funds are needed.

Request change of address to your address if decedent was receiving mail elsewhere.

Inquire about outstanding loans: get date-of-death principal and accrued interest balances and determine whether there was life insurance covering the loan.

B. Open an estate checking account.

To provide readily available money for meeting estate responsibilities and to establish an effective way of keeping estate records separate from all others, you probably will want to put some of the decedent's funds into a checking account in the name "The Estate of...." If you are the spouse and the entire estate goes to you, and if there is no question of adequacy of estate funds to meet all estate liabilities, this may not be necessary. Even in this case, however, there may be children or others for whom you will feel more comfortable to have clear and separate accounting.

Whether you choose an interest-bearing account might depend on how long it will take to settle the estate. At some point, a non-interest-bearing account can provide an advantage. By closing all other accounts and moving funds from matured or closed investments to this checking account, you can stop interest income on the entire estate. Stopping this income is the only way to stop receiving 1099's and possibly having to file another tax return, and the estate must not be closed with taxes due.

If you hire a lawyer, ask the bank to provide him or her with copies of checks and statements.

C. Collect all debts.

Collect rent, tax refunds, loan payments and other debts due the decedent. (GS28A-15 covers what portion of a tax refund belongs to spouse, what part to the estate.) If you encounter difficulties making collections, keep records of each contact, legal advice received, etc.

D. Collect all insurance.

Submit the decedent's claims for costs of doctors, prescriptions, hospital, home-health-care equipment, etc., to health insurance companies or Medicare.

Investigate benefits from all life, accident, cancer and other insurance policies. (Check with mortgage and loan companies and with credit card companies to see if life insurance policies covered debts owed to them.) Check policies for double-indemnity and other significant clauses. Ask insurance companies (or local agents) about procedure for collecting benefits; follow their instructions. Keep copies of all policies submitted.

Make beneficiaries aware of options for receiving insurance proceeds.

Check to see if any premium refunds are due; but before any policies are canceled, check the possibilities of continuing coverage for survivors and evaluate the pros and cons.

E. Look for and apply for other benefits.

Don't expect them to come automatically.

Apply for any survivor benefits available from the Social Security Administration. These include a small lump-sum death payment to the spouse and possibly other benefits for the spouse and dependent children. According to the benefit applied for, you may need the decedent's social security number, W-2 form, the spouse's and children's social security numbers, marriage license, divorce papers, birth certificates, adoption papers, etc. Don't delay applying if you don't have all of these, however. Social security employees may be able help you get what you need. (If you haven't already done so, stop any benefit payments to the decedent.) You may want the social security booklet, "Survivors." For questions not answered by a local social security office, call 1-800-772-1213.

Read employment agreements the decedent may have had. Check with the employer, and in some cases former employers, to see if any salary payments are due — including commissions, bonuses, and pay for unused vacation or sick leave. Ask about pension payments, insurance plans and other benefits. If the decedent was self-employed, check on possible private pension plans.

Apply for any veteran's benefits that might be due.

Don't overlook trade, professional, travel groups and clubs to which the decedent belonged. Contact each and inquire about insurance policies or other benefits.

Benefits that a spouse receives may be taxable; some may be eligible for rollover into an IRA. You would be wise to check with a tax authority about getting the best tax advantage.

F. Transact business related to real property.

Be sure that property insurance on buildings is adequate and in force for duration of the settlement process.

Establish values for 90-Day Inventory and/or tax returns.

If money is owed on property, don't pay without asking a lawyer whether the estate is liable for any part of that debt.

Unless by authority of a will, don't sell, lease or mortgage any real property without approval of the clerk.

If it is determined to be in the estate's best interest to sell real property, you must get approval from the clerk and follow the procedure required by law. (GS28A-15-l; GS28A-l 7-I through GS28A-17-13) If the property is in North Carolina, the clerk in your county can guide you. If it is in another state, check with the clerk in county of location.

Check to see if any deed changes need to be made. Real estate jointly owned by decedent and spouse as tenants in the entirety will pass directly to the spouse; the name on the deed does not have to be changed. (Such property does not have to be sold in order to satisfy the decedent's debts even if other resources have been depleted.) Other real property passes immediately to its heirs or, if devised in a will, to the devisees, and its value is not available to you unless you follow the procedure required to allow you to sell it if that is determined to be in the estate's best interest. (GS31-39)

G. Transact remaining business related to personal property.

Be sure property is secure and adequately insured, if applicable, during the settlement process.

Establish values for the 90-Day Inventory. You may need guidance. For instance, a nominal figure may be adequate for household furnishings, but a valuable coin collection to go to a nephew will need to be appraised. Sometimes a value is established by sale.

If personal property must be sold so you can satisfy claims or distribute the proceeds, you have that right, but don't sell household furnishings in the decedent's usual residence without checking with clerk or lawyer about timing. (GS28A-15 and 16).

If sale of business interests is involved, seek qualified counsel.

If the settlement is going to take considerable time, investigate possible investment opportunities for any cash not needed immediately and consider reinvestment options for maturing securities. But exercise extreme caution. Unless you are a skilled investor who is not grieving, seek advice from a trusted professional who has a proven investment record. Heartbreaking mistakes resulting in irrevocable losses are often made at this time. Offers, recommendations, promises of "great deals" may be heaped upon you, many from persons with good intentions, some from outright charlatans, but most people don't really know the investment world. Don't do anything without adequate investigation.

When it is determined that you no longer need control of property (Guideline 6), it may be transferred to the one entitled to it. You must get a signed receipt from beneficiaries or heirs for all property distributed. The receipt must state exactly what was received and accepted from the estate of_____ and it must be signed and dated. (Ask clerk if receipts are needed for household items not mentioned in the will). See Guideline 23 for sample wording if the distribution is the total or final share.

The nearest N.C. License Tag office will help you with vehicle title changes. Besides the title, you may need mileage on the vehicle, a fee, a Letter, a death certificate, and evidence of insurance.

Remind a surviving spouse to review his or her

estate plan, seeing that it takes into account any new property or other circumstances and that the decedent's name is removed as executor, trustee or beneficiary. The spouse also should re-evaluate insurance; more or less may be needed.

Have the decedent's name removed from insurance policies, credit cards, phone and water bills and other business accounts.

Intestate: If property goes to a minor child, the court may appoint someone to serve as guardian of the child's rights until the child reaches age 18.

If persons of quite differing needs and ideas share rights to property, there can sometimes be very emotional encounters related to necessary decisions. In such circumstances, a lawyer's meeting with the parties to clarify rights and discuss options may be essential — or parties may need to go before a mediator or arbitrator. A pattern of open, honest communication, established early in the process, should stand you well in such situations.

12. File the 90-Day Inventory with the clerk of court. (GS28A-20)

This inventory is to be an accurate inventory of the decedent's property as of the date of death. It is to include descriptions and values of both real and personal property, including interest or dividends, where applicable, accrued to the date of death.

Clarifications given earlier, in Guideline 2, concerning what portion of an asset is probate property, also apply here. Court fees will be figured on the value of probate property shown on this inventory.

For accounts, give the name of the financial institution, account names and numbers. For securities, also show number and kind of shares.

List each vehicle and other significant tangible assets (valuable collections, rare items, etc.) separately. If the estate is going to pay a debt on a vehicle, don't subtract the debt amount when determining vehicle value. If the debt is going to be assumed by the recipient, you may subtract the outstanding debt before arriving at the probate asset value.

List "household furnishings" and a value for the whole, not individual items. Unless family disagreements force appraisals, this is usually sufficient.

If there is real property, identify it by address, acreage, Deed Book and page number if possible.

If an asset was appraised, give the appraiser's name and address. If it has been impossible to arrive at a value, the clerk may allow it to be listed "to be determined" and give you a bit more time.

If you did not submit them with the preliminary inventory, attach, or take with you, copies of signature cards or deposit contracts for all joint accounts. You may also need proofs of balances held.

Disbursements and additions *since* the date of death are *not* included on this accounting; they will be reflected on the Annual or Final account.

Some clerks will send a bill for the [fee]. Some will want payment at the [time of the inventory].

If you later discover an error or omission, you may have to submit a supplemental inventory or you may be able to reflect corrections on the next accounting.

Ask for the form you need for next reporting

("Annual or Final Account"). If you will need AOC-E-212 or AOC-E-207 (Guideline 17) also get that form.

13. Send notice of fiduciary relationship to IRS.

You are acting in a fiduciary capacity, and IRS must have a written notice of your legal appointment. The notice should be filed as soon as all of the necessary information (including the EIN) is available. It must precede or accompany the first federal return filed. With it, you must send a Letter Testamentary or Letter of Administration. Form 56 is provided as a convenience. Though its use is not required, it will assure that your notice includes all necessary information and may help with routing and documentation in the IRS's labyrinth of paperwork. (You may also use Form 56 when notifying IRS that your fiduciary relationship has ended, Guideline 25.)

14. File decedent's state and federal income tax returns for the year prior to year of death, if the returns have not been filed. (Likely to be necessary if the death was before April 15.)

The method of filing (jointly or singly) and information included will be exactly as it would have been if the death had not occurred. "Deceased" and date of death should be written at top of return beside the name.

No matter when the date of death, returns are [due on time] and a penalty will be charged if they are late. Dependence on an attorney or an accountant to do returns is no excuse. You are responsible for meeting deadlines. Even if no taxes must be paid, a return should be filed if a refund is due.

IRS Publication 17, "Your Federal Income Tax," can be helpful in filing these returns.

IRS Form 4810, "Request for Prompt Assessment," can be filed after the income tax return has been filed. This request will usually reduce the time, from 3 years to 18 months, in which the IRS can charge additional taxes. This may permit earlier settlement and final distribution of assets.

These are not the final individual income tax returns — the final ones are for the actual year of death.

15. Pay debts and claims.

Before paying anything, carefully review priorities for payments in Guideline 6. Most claims submitted after the published deadline do not have to be paid.

Utility bills incurred after the death are the responsibility of the beneficiary of the property.

A lawyer's fee may need approval by the clerk before it is paid.

16. File the decedent's final state and federal income tax returns.

These are the returns for the final year of the decedent's life. "Deceased" and date of death should be written at the top beside the name. Returns are due on the [date] they would have been due if the decedent had lived. Relying on a lawyer or accountant to do returns is no excuse for being late; penalties will be charged for failure to meet deadlines. Payment of estimated taxes is not required after death, but be sure payments have been adequate to avoid penalties.

Even if death was early in the year and income was insufficient to require payment of taxes, a zero-balance return should be submitted in order to avoid confusion and possible penalty charges. If taxes were withheld or estimated taxes paid, a return must be filed if a refund is to be received.

IRS Form 4810, "Request for Prompt Assessment," may be filed after the income tax return is filed. It may reduce from 3 years to 18 months the time in which IRS can assess additional taxes.

IRS Publication 559, "Tax Information for Survivors, Executors, and Administrators," is an essential reference for the federal return. It also lists federal returns, other than those on the checklist, that are sometimes required.

Have your tax authority determine whether taxes other than those on the checklist might be due at any time during the settlement process.

17. File N.C. estate tax return OR tax certification.

In 1998, our General Assembly did away with the "N.C. inheritance tax" on estates of those dying after Jan. 1, 1999, and simultaneously enacted a new "Estate Tax." (GS105-1A)

This new N.C. tax is imposed on an estate only if the estate is subject to the *federal* estate tax imposed under section 2001 of the Internal Revenue Code.

This means that under the new law, no N.C. estate tax will be due unless the total value of the taxable estate is greater than the exclusion amount listed on chart on next page:

In the case of estates of decedents dying, and gifts made, during:	The applicable exclusion amount is:
1999	$ 650,000
2000 and 2001	675,000
2002 and 2003	700,000
2004	850,000
2005	950,000
2006 (and, as of now, thereafter)	1,000,000

If no N.C. estate taxes are due, you must complete the tax certification form, AOC-E-212, and file it with the clerk. (This form is available from the clerk).

If the gross value of the estate exceeds the exclusion amount, the N.C. Tax Return (A-101) must be filed with the N.C. Department of Revenue. It is a simple form that requires figures from the federal return. The [date] by which it must be filed is the same as the date by which the U.S. estate tax return must be filed.

You are allowed to sell estate assets in order to pay this tax. (GS105-32.4) Check with clerk or attorney before selling.

The PR can be liable for any estate tax not paid within two years after it was due. (GS28A-8)

If you are working with the estate of someone who died before Jan. 1, 1999, you must determine whether inheritance taxes are due. If not, you must complete the form AOC-E-207 and file it with the clerk. If you need to file the tax return, it is A-100, "North Carolina Inheritance and Estate Tax."

18. File United States estate tax return, if necessary.

If the gross value of the estate plus any adjusted taxable gifts is more than the exclusion amount shown in Guideline 17, this return, Form 706, must be filed. (For a death in 1998, the filing requirement was $625,000. Prior to that it was $600,000).

The gross estate includes the value of all property in which the decedent held an interest at the time of death. It also includes life insurance payable to the estate or, if the decedent was the owner, to beneficiaries, and includes the value of certain annuities and certain property transferred within three years prior to death.

Taking full advantage of the unified credit and other allowable deductions will require the services of a tax authority. Expertise is also essential because the PR can be liable for estate taxes. Filing the return may not mean taxes due.

The EIN must go on the return.

Form 4810, "Request for Prompt Assessment," may be filed.

IRS Publication 448, "Federal Estate and Gift Taxes," and Publication 950, "Introduction to Estate and Gift Taxes," are essential references for this return. Other forms and publications may also apply to your situation.

If you discover that the decedent made gifts in excess of $10,000 to any one donee within a taxable year, study IRS publication 448 and talk with your tax professional to determine whether you need to file form 709, "United States Gift Tax Return."

If you must file a gift tax return, figure the [due date] and write in an additional line on your Checklist. At this writing, there is continuing debate about the repeal of the N.C. gift tax. If a federal return is required, and if N.C. still has a gift tax, the N.C. return must also be filed.

Testate: A certified copy of the will, available from the clerk, must accompany the U.S. estate tax return.

19. Receive tax clearance.

If it was necessary to file federal and N.C. estate tax returns, you must receive clearance (closing letter or notification that the estate tax liability has been satisfied) from both U.S. and N.C. Departments of Revenue before distribution of the estate can be completed.

A copy of the federal Closing Letter must be filed with the N.C. Department of Revenue promptly after its receipt. (IRS may require a copy of N.C.'s notification).

The clerk is likely to require seeing both notices.

20. File federal and state fiduciary income tax returns, if necessary.

The estate is a taxable entity that comes into being with the death of the decedent and remains in existence until final distribution of its assets. If the estate has a year's gross income that exceeds [the amount set by law], you must file Form 1041, "U.S. Fiduciary Income Tax Return." The state form is D-407. Whether or not earnings exceed that amount, a return may need to be filed for a year in which income is distributed.

Beneficiaries' or heirs' social security numbers may be required.

Taxes may be figured on the total income and be paid from the estate before the beneficiaries' shares of the income are distributed, or all the interest may be distributed and tax responsibility be passed on to the beneficiaries.

You must choose whether to use calendar or fiscal year as the basis for filing this return. Date of death will determine which is most advantageous. If the date was near the beginning of the year, calendar year may work well. For a later death date, choosing a fiscal year with month-prior-to-month-of-death as its end (to allow a full year before it's due), may prevent having to file more than one fiduciary return.

The EIN must go on the federal return.

Publication 559, "Tax Information for Survivors, Executors, and Administrators," is an essential reference for this return.

Form 4810, "Request for Prompt Assessment," may be filed.

If federal fiduciary tax returns must be filed for more than two years, estimated tax payments are required beginning the third year of estate settlement.

21. File Annual Account with the clerk, if necessary. (GS28A-21)

If the Final Account has not been filed, then an Annual Account must be filed by its [deadline]. One must be submitted every year until the Final Account is filed.

On the first Annual Account, begin with the balance from the 90-Day Inventory and then show all additions to and disbursements from that balance, including losses/gains (from sales, for example, or on investments).

If any property considered a non-probate asset for the 90-Day Inventory has been used for paying debts and claims, it must be listed as a receipt. It should be equaled by disbursements.

The clerk must see canceled checks or other proof for all payments, proofs of balances being held or invested, receipts for any distributions to beneficiaries or heirs.

A [fee] will be charged.

The Annual Account will be audited by the clerk and you will be notified as to its acceptance.

22. Determine net shares due beneficiaries or heirs.

Net shares are figured from value remaining, if any, after all additions have been included and all estate obligations mentioned in Guideline 6 have been subtracted. If other taxes or any other debts or claims remain on the estate, you cannot yet determine final net share figures. (Remember to allow for fees that will be due with Annual and/or Final accounting.)

For many estates, the final figures can be illusive. PR's often make distribution in more than one installment, being sure to hold back, for awhile, enough money to safeguard against unforeseen liabilities. (For instance, it takes the government considerable time to review returns and determine whether more taxes are due.) If such money is held back, it should be reported to beneficiaries along with the explanation that these funds or a report of their use will be sent to them after a specified time.

Plan carefully to have funds available when needed for distribution. You don't want to liquidate securities earlier than you need to and lose more interest than necessary, but you don't want to leave funds earning interest so long that you will have 1099's and additional tax returns beyond your projected estate closure deadline.

Intestate: Property that was given as an advancement during the lifetime of the decedent is to be counted toward the recipient's share; if it exceeded his or her intestate share, the recipient won't have to return any of what was received from the decedent but will be excluded from receiving anything more. (GS29-23) (An "advancement" means that it was intended by the decedent to enable the recipient to anticipate his or her inheritance to the extent of the gift.)

23. Complete the distribution of the estate to beneficiaries or heirs.

If there is reason to question readiness for final accounting at this point, you might want to prepare a preliminary Final Account to show the clerk, if the clerk is willing, for approval or guidance before making final distribution.

When everything due to the estate has been received and all estate liabilities have been provided for, remaining assets must be distributed according to the will, if there is one, or according to the Intestate Succession Act, GS29 (see Chapter 5). If property goes to a minor, or if a beneficiary owed a debt to the decedent, investigate options.

Get a receipt for each distribution. It should make clear that everything due from the estate has been received. Unless the clerk provided a form or wording, consider this sample: "I have received and accepted_____ from the estate of _____ and acknowledge that this is my total (or "final," whichever applies) share of this estate." Include spaces for date and signature. If you want the receipt notarized, that should also be indicated. (When preparing the form, you should fill in the blank which specifies what you are distributing and fill in the decedent's name after "estate of.") If distribution is by check, the receipt wording may be placed on the back of the check above the endorsement. Ask the clerk if this would serve as the only necessary receipt or just a backup.

24. File the Final Account with the clerk of court. (GS28A-21-1,3)

If all debts and claims have been satisfied and the other duties completed, the Final Account may be filed at any time after the date specified in the notice to creditors. However, it *must* be filed by its [deadline] unless an extension has been granted by the clerk. (In some cases, several extensions must be granted.)

This account must show all additions and disbursements since the last accounting. If any property considered a non-probate asset for the last accounting has been used for paying debts and claims, it must be listed as a receipt. It should be equaled by disbursements.

The clerk must see canceled checks or other proof of payments and you must provide receipts for all distributions to beneficiaries or heirs.

A [fee] will be charged.

When the clerk receives and approves the Final Account, the clerk will enter an order discharging you from further liability.

(If other property or the omission of some task should later be discovered, the estate can be reopened.)

25. Notify IRS of termination of your fiduciary relationship.

Use Form 56 for this purpose. With the notice, send proof of the termination of your responsibilities.

This notice should be sent promptly.

Chapter 5

Distribution of Property for One Who Died Intestate

The General Statutes which determine the heirs and what they will receive are GS29-14 through GS29-30. They are quite detailed and cover rights of individuals in every possible relationship to the decedent. For some estates, the determination of heirs and their rights is very simple. For others, it can be a complex matter requiring a lawyer's work. Check facts and calculations with an authority before distributing property.

Refer to Chapter 6 for amounts to go in the blanks in B, C, and D.

A surviving spouse considering the life estate option, briefly described at the end of the chart, should discuss advantages and disadvantages with a lawyer.

A surviving spouse who is considering dissenting from a will in order to claim the intestate share will also need clarification of rights. Under some circumstances, they are not the same as those indicated.

Second spouse's rights are not always the same as those of the first spouse.

	If Heirs are:	Their share of the net estate will be:
A	A spouse but no lineal descendants or parents	100 percent
B	A spouse* (see note at end of chart)	$_____,000 of personalty plus one-half of balance of personalty and one-half of realty
	and one child	the remainder
	or lineal descendants of one deceased child •	the deceased child's share divided as explained for grandchildren and succeeding generations in (C) below
C	A spouse* (see note at end of chart)	$_____,000 of personalty plus one-third of balance of personalty and one-third of realty
	and two or more children	to figure shares of living children: divide remaining estate by no. of living plus no. of deceased children who left lineal descendants
	and/or lineal descendants of two or more deceased children	to figure shares for grandchildren by deceased children: divide any remaining estate by no. of living plus no. of deceased grandchildren who left lineal descendants (same process for next generation)

	If Heirs are:	Their share of the net estate will be:
D	A spouse * (see note at end of chart) (no lineal descendants) and decedent's parent(s)	$_____ 000 of personalty plus one-half of balance of personalty and one-half of realty the remainder
E	(no spouse) lineal descendants	the total estate: see explanation in (C) above to determine shares
F	(no spouse or lineal descendants) decedent's parents	100 percent
G	(no spouse, lineal descendants or parents) brothers and sisters and/or lineal descendants of brothers and sisters	to figure shares of living brothers/sisters: divide estate by no. of living plus no. of deceased brothers/sisters who left lineal descendants to figure shares of living nieces/nephews by deceased brothers/sisters: divide any remaining estate by no. of living nieces/nephews plus no.of deceased nieces/nephews who left lineal descendants (same process for next generation)

	If Heirs are:	Their share of the net estate will be:
H	(no spouse, lineal descendants, brothers/sisters, or lineal descendants of brothers/sisters) paternal grandparent(s), if living, otherwise to paternal aunts and uncles and lineal descendants of deceased paternal aunts and uncles (if none, this share passes as part of the share described immediately below	one-half
	maternal grandparent(s), if living, otherwise to maternal aunts and uncles and lineal descendants of deceased maternal aunts and uncles (if none, this share passes as part of the share described immediately above)	one half

*A surviving spouse who is not entitled to the entire net estate has some options.

The spouse may elect to take a life estate instead of the intestate share. According to my interpretation of GS29-30, a surviving spouse may choose to take a life estate in one of two ways.

Unless the surviving spouse previously has waived or released his or her rights to such property, he or she may take a life estate in one third in value of all the real estate which the decedent had which was capable of being passed on in an inheritance.

Or, regardless of the value, the surviving spouse may elect to take a life estate in the usual dwelling house occupied by him or her at the time of the death of the decedent if such dwelling were owned by the decedent at the time of his or her death, together with the outbuildings, improvements and easements belonging or pertaining to them, and lands upon which they are situated and which are reasonably necessary for their use and enjoyment, as well as a fee simple ownership in the household furnishings therein.

There is a [deadline for making this election]. The election must be filed with the clerk of court.

Taking a life estate means that the spouse's rights to the property last for only his or her lifetime. He or she cannot then leave the property by will or trust, etc., to others.

Chapter 6

Deadlines, Fees and Values Set by Law

Laws change. Don't assume you know what they are. Though many stay the same for years, they are subject to amendment. Don't rely on any deadlines or other estate-related figures you have heard or read about, here or elsewhere, without first checking with an authority.

Authorities

The clerk of superior court can serve as your authority for inventories, accountings, deadlines, fees and most other figures on these pages except those having to do with taxes.

A qualified lawyer is your authority for interpretation of laws and their application to your circumstances. He or she may also serve as your authority for inventories, accountings, deadlines and most other matters addressed in this book.

A qualified accountant or N.C. Department of Revenue and IRS employees, or current tax publications can serve as your authority for tax deadlines and for other tax information.

Deadlines

Guide-line No.	Action/Responsibility	Due
1	Dissent must be filed by spouse or his/her lawyer	Within 6 months of PR's qualification
2	Qualified person must inventory lockbox	Before anything can be removed
5	Publish creditors' notice	Promptly after qualification
5	Deadline (to put in notice) by which claims must be submitted	At least 3 months from 1st publication
5	Send copy of notice to known creditors	Within 75 days of qualification
10	Allowances are to be paid	Within the first year following decedent's death
12	File 90-day inventory	Within 90 days of qualification unless extension granted
13	Send notice of fiduciary relationship	Promptly — must precede or accompany first IRS return filed as PR
14	File decedent's year-prior-to-year-of-death state and federal returns, if not already filed	April 15, year of death
16	File decedent's final state and federal returns	April 15, year after year of death

Deadlines

Guide-line No.	Action/Responsibility	Due
17	File N.C. estate tax return or tax certification	Due 9 months after the date of decedent's death
18	File federal estate tax return	Due 9 months after date of decedent's death
18	If gift tax due	On April 15 of year following year in which gift was made — or due date for estate return, whichever is earlier
20	File fiduciary returns	Due 3 1/2 months after end of taxable year
21	File annual account with clerk of court	Within one year of qualification, and annually thereafter until final account is filed.

Deadlines

Guide-line No.	Action/Responsibility	Due
24	File final account with clerk of court	Any time which is after the date specified in the notice to creditors and within 12 months of qualification (unless an extension is granted)

Additional deadlines — Intestate only

Guide-line No.	Action/Responsibility	Due
9	Spouse may elect life estate in lieu of intestate share	Within one month after date in notice to creditors, if Letters are issued within 12 months of decedent's death. If Letters have not been issued, election must be made within 12 months of death of deceased spouse. If litigation pending, then according to timing ordered by clerk.

Fees, charges and values

Guide-line No.	Job	Fee or charge
2	Clerk's inventory of lockbox (rarely needed)	$15
2	Drilling of lockbox	$100 (or more)
3	Facilities and qualification fees* (usually paid at time of 90-Day Inventory)	$36
3	Cost of Letters Testamentary or of Administration	$1 each over 5
4	Death certificates	$3 each
6	In priority class No. 2, if funds are not adequate for all bills, the limit allowable for funeral expenses (Claims in other classes may also have to be prorated)	$2,500
6	Maximum percent of receipts and disbursements allowed for PR's fee if justified by circumstances	5%
7	Penalty for omitting EIN from federal returns	$50
12	Costs due at time of 90-Day Inventory: on value of personal property minimum charge maximum charge	40¢ per $100 $10 $3,000
21/24	Fee charged on new value shown on annual and final accounts is figured the same as for 90-day inventory — but if less than $2,500 new value, or if maximum of $3,000 has been paid*	$10

* If a trust was established under a will, there may be additional fees related to it.

Other money amounts

Guide-line No.	Item	Amount
10	Spouse allowance	$10,000
10	Allowance for each eligible child	$2,000
20	Fiduciary Taxes (taxes on income earned by the estate) are paid if in any one year the estate earns more than	$600

Intestate only
(Above money amounts and fees/charges also apply)

See chart in chap-ter 5	Spouse's specified portion of personalty in (B)	$30,000
	Spouse's specified portion of personalty in (C)	$30,000
	Spouse's specified portion of personalty in (D)	$50,000

Appendix A

Record Keeping

You must keep copies of all canceled checks, statements, receipts, incoming and outgoing correspondence, every bit of data pertaining to the estate, because: (1) the clerk of court will require validation of every disbursement from the estate and may ask for verification of any entry on accountings, and (2) the information is essential for tax returns.

Accurate, complete, easily-accessible files and notes can also save you from costly mistakes, wasted time and considerable frustration related to other tasks.

For instance, one savings and loan company employee with whom I worked lost my entire file. My copies of correspondence proved that I had met all requirements; she was most apologetic but never found the file. I had to provide duplicates of several documents as well as of the correspondence.

Shortly after that, another institution declared that I had never sent the death certificate and other necessary paperwork. I quoted the date and body of the letter which had accompanied those documents and evidence of the institution's response. Those papers were eventually found, filed under my name rather than under the estate's name where they belonged.

Establish a file, portable if possible. (Being able to carry it means having everything available at your fingertips when going to banks, clerk of court, etc. and may save trips. I've used a zippered bag from the funeral home.) Consider the following as beginning file captions: Bills/Claims; Correspondence; Estate Checking Account; Inventories/Accountings; Investments (or a separate folder for each investment); Receipts; Taxes (or a separate folder for each type return).

Get a spiral or small looseleaf notebook in which to record work you do and numbers you need for easy reference. Inside the cover or on the first page write the decedent's date of birth, date of death, social security number, medicare/insurance number(s), address at death. Also write the date of your qualification, the estate's tax ID (employer identification number — EIN) and the file number the clerk put at the top of your approved application for probate (this number should be referred to on future filings and correspondence with the clerk of court.)

Establish a page for phone numbers. As you call clerk, accountant, attorney, investment institutions, jot the numbers here so they're quickly available next time.

Set aside pages for recording information gathered by phone and for keeping other significant notes. Be sure to record every step taken to collect debts, any professional advice received/date/from whom, other input from family members and beneficiaries.

If you expect reimbursement from the estate for

expenses, or if you feel it might be helpful to the clerk in determining your fee, you may want to prepare pages with columns such as: Date; Work Done; Time; Mileage; Phone Calls; Other Expenses.

Appendix B

Lawyers and Accountants

When you need a lawyer or accountant, what are your primary concerns? "Fees" and "finding a good one" are common responses to that question. This chapter shares some information about fees and suggests ways to find one of N.C.'s many fine attorneys and accountants who are committed to excellence. It also suggests ways to establish effective communication that should prevent surprises and provide the foundation for a solid working relationship.

As background for addressing the matter of lawyers' fees, consider this statement from the "Estate Procedures Pamphlet" from the N.C. Administrative Office of the Courts: "The personal representative may choose to hire an attorney. However, the funds of the estate may not be used to pay the attorney's fees unless the clerk finds that the fee is reasonable. Unless the attorney's services are beyond the normal scope of estate administration, the attorney's fees allowed may reduce the amount of the personal representative's commission." (AOC-B0021, Rev. 10/95, pg. 6)

The PR's commission is what I've called, in

Guideline 6, the PR's "fee" of up to 5 percent of receipts and disbursements. That fee, or commission, is for doing the work of estate administration. Complexity of the work and time required are considered by the clerk who determines the fee.

The statement from AOC seems to say that if the administration of a particular estate requires some work that is *beyond* the normal scope of the PR's job, the clerk will approve use of estate funds to pay a reasonable fee to an attorney for doing that work — and such payment will *not* affect the PR's potential commission. If, however, the PR chooses to hire an attorney to do part of the work that is normally considered *within* the scope of the PR's job, then a reasonable fee paid to the attorney for that work *may* reduce the commission paid to the PR. I interpret AOC's words to reflect a desire to see that estate funds are used to justly compensate both the attorney and the PR — each for the work s/he actually did — and to avoid compensating either of them for work done by the other.

If an attorney takes the oath and is appointed as PR, then the clerk can approve use of estate funds to pay that attorney both the PR's commission and a fee for any work beyond the usual routine of the PR's job, work for which any other PR would be reasonably justified in hiring legal counsel (GS28A-23-4).

(A High Point attorney shared his understanding that if the will specifically allows the PR to hire an attorney to assist, then the attorney's fee is not subject to court approval.)

It is important, then, to understand what share of the work only you can, or want, to do and what portion you may need to hire someone to do. A few questions in Chapter 1 and a look at the Checklist, Chapter 3, may help you evaluate what you want to do, have time to do and/or are capable of doing.

It's also important to realize that both lawyers' and accountants' charges vary widely and are influenced by training and expertise, reputation, location, office overhead, etc. They may also sometimes be influenced by the professional's perception of the client — whether the client will be able and willing to cooperate in an efficient, responsible manner, for instance, or whether the work is likely to involve disorganized information and unnecessary hassles or frustrations dumped into the professional's lap. In other words, fees are not set in law nor in stone.

According to the best information I could get, the range of N.C. lawyers' hourly rates is approximately $75 to $250. Some attorneys may suggest a charge of a percentage of the estate rather than a charge of an hourly rate. If payment of a percentage of the estate is suggested, be aware of several crucial issues:

(a) Both parties must understand whether you're discussing a percentage of the taxable estate or of only the probate property. As discussed elsewhere, those two figures are likely to be very different because the taxable estate may include real estate, insurance, annuities, etc., that are not ordinarily part of the estate that is subject to probate.

(b) You should be sure, before agreeing to pay a percentage of *any* part of the estate, that you have a clear concept of the estate's total value and what that percentage is likely to represent. At the beginning of the work, a PR often is not fully aware of all the property and therefore can't know the total value of either the probate estate or the taxable estate.

(c) The size of the estate does not directly determine the amount of work required. If the estate is large, but requires minimum time, risk and work, a charge of a percentage could be unfair to the estate. On the other hand, payment of a percentage of a small estate that involves time-consuming entanglements could be unfair to the lawyer.

One highly respected attorney with whom I talked (highest *Martindale-Hubbell Law Directory* rating) suggested that one valid way to use a percentage might be to consider an agreement in which an hourly charge is set with the understanding that total charges cannot exceed an agreed-upon percentage (1 percent to 5 percent). Again, be sure there's a clear understanding of whether the percentage is of the probate property of the estate or of the total, taxable estate.

Another attorney, in a large firm that monitors charges, said the attorneys there charge by the hour and their total charges have usually been found to fall in a range that equals 1 percent to 1 1/2 percent of the total, taxable estate.

I discovered that accountants' fees cover as wide a range as those charged by attorneys. Within one three-week period, I showed two accountants, both with excellent credentials, identical work. One estimated his total charge would be $4,000 to $8,000; the other estimated a charge of $200 to $400.

When considering the services for which you will

pay an accountant, remember that their fees are to be based only on work related to preparing returns. It is the unauthorized practice of law for accountants to advise on legal matters other than tax work, so don't ask that of them nor accept that from them.

Neither "cheaper" nor "more expensive" is a sure guarantee of a better deal. The person who charges $150 per hour may be better trained or more efficient and may complete the work in half the time taken by the person who charges $75 per hour, thereby actually not charging more in the long run and saving time and stress, too. On the other hand, the one who charges less may also be just as efficient and just as well trained and may save the estate money.

In the above situation, I gave the work to the accountant who gave the lower estimate. He was very pleasant to work with, and the charge for the completed work was $350. I did discover, by studying IRS publication 559, that he had failed to use a deduction which would have saved the estate about $2,000. He filed, without charge, an amended return. In this case, his services would have saved the estate $1,650 to $5,650 even if I had not caught the deduction.

Beyond the point about fees, the discovery of the omission serves as good supporting evidence for one of the theories behind this book: two heads are better than one even when one of the heads belongs to a nonprofessional. Even the best-trained mind is also dealing with stresses of everyday life and may sometimes make an error or miss something significant.

The accountant, by the way, who gave the higher estimate, was recommended by a professional friend I greatly respect. In our free get-acquainted session, his very forthright answers to every question revealed him to be an unusually meticulous, methodical worker, and he was part of a sizable and well-established accounting firm. If a client had work bound to present some sort of complex challenge, that accountant's approach and the availability of on-sight counsel from other members of the firm might merit consideration.

In other words, carefully evaluate fee amounts, but also do your best to understand your needs and to adequately investigate a much broader scope of credentials of the person you are considering hiring.

Look carefully at what your money will be buying. The amount of the fee is not, in itself, a guarantee of the presence or absence of expertise, efficiency, honesty, professionalism and consideration for the client. Fee totals will strongly influence your ultimate satisfaction or distress, but so will the professional's unique measure of the above qualities in relationship to your needs and to your own unique blend of attitude and efficiency.

Lawyers

How to Find a Good Lawyer and Establish Effective Communication:

1. Confine your consideration to lawyers with special certification for probate work or to those with verifiable records of considerable probate experience and standards of excellence. A brochure on finding the right lawyer, available from the North Carolina State Bar Board of Legal Specialization, explains that to be certified a lawyer must: be an active member in good

standing of the North Carolina State Bar for at least five years; pass a written examination in the area of specialty; devote at least 25 percent of his or her practice to the specialty during the past five years; attend continuing legal education seminars; and be favorably evaluated by other lawyers and judges. The brochure further says that only one so certified is entitled to advertise as a specialist certified by the North Carolina State Bar. It also offers a free directory of names, addresses and phone numbers of all lawyers so certified (919-828-4620, Ext. 249)

a. Listen to what your acquaintances say about lawyers whose estate work has pleased them, and let that be one factor to consider — but know that you cannot possibly, in that way alone, get a whole picture of what is available to you. Remember, too, that the work you need done will be somewhat different from that needed by most every other person you talk with and that your personality may relate quite differently to a particular individual.

b. You can go to the research section of your library and ask for help in finding the N.C. volume of the *Martindale-Hubbell Law Directory*. This book contains quite a bit of information about lawyers in your area. It may take a bit of time to understand the meaning of some of the codes, some of which are keyed to other sections of the volume, and look up related data, but there are user's helps in the front of the volume. There is also an alphabetical listing of lawyers, by city, with abbreviations indicating the firms with which they are associated. In some cases, this same listing will show a rating, by other lawyers, of that attorney's ability and character. (If, for example, an AV appears after the name, the A indicates the highest rating for legal ability; the V indicates very high integrity and character. The lack of a rating may not, however, indicate the lack of these desired qualifications. (It may simply mean the attorney has not practiced long enough or is not gregarious enough to be well known by his or her peers or that ratings had not been received and processed by publication deadline.) There is information about educational background and area of expertise, plus a biographical professional section of the book which is broken down by city and law firms.

c. You can call the North Carolina State Bar in Raleigh, 919-828-4620, and learn whether there have ever been charges against a particular attorney that have reached the "probable cause" level of seriousness or if public disciplinary action has ever been taken against the attorney. (The North Carolina State Bar is an organization to which every N.C. lawyer must belong. It is the body that regulates admission to the practice of law, is responsible for dealing with charges and for taking disciplinary action. It is not the same as the North Carolina Bar Association, in which membership is voluntary and the purposes of which are entirely different.)

d. You can go to the courthouse and look through probate files, the files of estate settlement records for your county. These are public records, meaning they are readily available to you. You can review a lawyer's work by looking at accountings to the clerk and can see what fee was paid to him or her. To find a file, you will need to know the name of some of those whose estates the lawyer has worked with or the names of some devisees. Look, first, for the big books, *Wills* and *Devisees*. In *Wills*, you can find the file number of the person whose will was probated or whose estate was administered in the absence of a will. *Devisees* gives the file numbers of those to whom property was devised. When you have found the file number you want, you can then ask if you should go to the file room yourself or if someone should pull the file for you.

e. If you need to talk with a lawyer just briefly, you may call the N.C. Bar Association Lawyer Referral Service, 1-800-662-7660, describe your need and any selection criteria you consider significant, and be given the name of a lawyer to whom you may talk for 30 minutes for (as of this writing) $30. This service is intended to provide legal help for a specific concern. You may, as a by-product, gain insight into whether this is someone you might want to hire for further help, but this is not intended as a get-acquainted session in which you are determining whom you want to hire to do longer-range work. For that need, most attorneys offer a free session in which you may ask questions such as those suggested under 2-b.

f. Some cities have local bar referral services. To check, look in your phone book under the name of the city followed by Bar Referral Service.

g. If you are a senior citizen, check with your local Council on Aging or other senior services agencies to see if they can assist you with information or referral.

h. You might consider that the decedent's choice of a particular attorney to draw his or her will may have indicated the decedent's confidence in that attorney.

2. Choose the name of an attorney you are very seriously considering, then:

a. Call and see if she or he offers a free get-acquainted session. Most do. This is not a time in which to get free legal advice but a time for asking questions which will help you evaluate the attorney's qualifications and get a sense of the likelihood for a good working relationship. You may want to take a member of the decedent's family with you to help listen, take notes, and ask questions.

b. Take the following to the get-acquainted session: a list of those who will benefit from the estate, the will (if there is one), and what you know at this point of the estate's assets and liabilities. Also take a list of the questions you want to ask — a list on which you have left room for noting answers. You should ask any or all of the following:

• Are you certified specifically for probate/estate work?

• Approximately what percentage of your case load is devoted to estate work?

• Approximately how many estates have you handled in the past five years?

• If we work together, is it agreeable with you for me to do all of the work I possibly can, having you available for advice and to handle steps I can't, or would you expect to handle all the work except gathering information, signings, etc., that only I can do?

• Will you provide me a list of references?

• What is your hourly fee? (If she or he should say a percentage of the estate rather than an hourly rate is charged, remember considerations mentioned in the introductory paragraphs. And do not accept answers such as, "We'll see as we get into the work," or "I usually just charge whatever the clerk allows," or "the fee allowed by law," etc. If you get such an answer and further questions do not bring complete and satisfactory understanding, don't consider hiring the attorney without further investigation.)

• Do you figure charges in increments of tenth or quarter hours? (This can result in lower total charges if there are many small increments of time involved — phone calls from or to you, notes dictated, etc.)

• If paralegals or other assistants do part of the work, is the charge less for their work? If so, what is the hourly charge for their work? (If you consider having the lawyer do the tax returns, ask specifically about the hourly rate for that work so you can compare with estimates you get from accountants.)

• Do you require a retainer (an upfront charge)? If so, what does it cover? Is the retainer an advance against total fees? (One attorney suggested that in the case of a very small estate it might be appropriate to require a retainer, but otherwise be wary of a request for a retainer unless the matter being handled involves litigation.)

• Will you give me, before we actually begin working, a written estimate of total charges — fees, phone calls, letters, etc.? Will you talk with me before exceeding such an estimate?

• If I ask that charges not exceed a specified amount without my written permission, would you agree to that?

• Will you give me a written estimate of time you

think the work will take? Will you inform me if it appears your time will exceed your estimate?

• If you routinely give estimates, do you most often underestimate or overestimate?

• Are you willing to consent to binding arbitration in the event of serious fee disagreement between us and to put this consent in writing?

• Do you prepare an engagement letter (contract), for both of us to sign, that states our understanding of fees, the work you commit to do, how any disputes between us would be handled, an estimate of how long the work will take? If you don't ordinarily prepare such engagement letters, will you be willing to in this case? (This is more and more a common practice and can avoid many problems.)

• Do you itemize bills and in your itemization will you include who did the work, his or her hourly charge, the actual time spent and a description of the work performed?

• How regularly will you keep me informed of progress on your work?

• From your experience with other clients, what suggestions would you make to me concerning ways I can best contribute to a good working relationship?

• In your experience with other clients, what have been their most common mistakes?

3. Evaluate the information you have gathered and be aware of your response to the person you have interviewed:

• Were your questions answered forthrightly? Were answers and explanations in vocabulary you could understand? Did the answers satisfy you? Will written fee and time estimates, engagement letter, itemized bills be available? If not, you should look elsewhere, at least for the sake of comparison, before hiring.

Did you sense this attorney to be open and approachable, or condescending, impatient? Did you experience a sense of confidence, trust? Though you cannot possibly have perfect perception of potential for a good working relationship, you will have picked up some valid indicators.

What to Do if Problems Arise
Between You and the Lawyer You Hire:

If, in spite of all the above, problems should arise, consider options mentioned below. If you need additional guidance, call your city or county bar association.

1. Serious charges against an attorney (embezzlement, for example) must be filed with and handled by the North Carolina State Bar, Raleigh: 919-828-4620.

2. Lesser charges or conflicts may be handled through a Judicial District Grievance Committee if the district in which the lawyer practices has such a committee. If the district does not have such a committee, then all complaints should be filed with the North Carolina State Bar.

3. Some judicial districts have arbitration panels before whom both parties may appear and work out voluntary but binding determinations, or rulings, when a fee is in dispute. (Some districts make arbitration rulings binding only on the attorney; some make them binding on both parties.)

Accountants

Some of the preceding information is applicable to your search for and communication with accountants. In addition, the following may be helpful.

1. If you choose a certified public accountant, you can know that he or she is required to have 40 hours of continuing professional education each year in order to maintain that certification. Even so, you will want to hire only one with specialized training or with considerable experience with estate returns. If you cannot locate such an accountant, you may contact the North Carolina Association of CPA's: 1-800-722-2836 or 919-469-1040. This organization has lists of accountants who concentrate in specialized areas.

2. Call the accountant you are considering and inquire about a free get-acquainted session. When you go for such a session, take information that will enable the accountant to get a good idea of the work involved. If you need individual income tax returns filed for the decedent, take a copy of his or her previous year's return and information about significant changes. If you will need N.C. estate tax and federal estate returns done, take the estate inventory and list of beneficiaries. If you will need fiduciary returns, take information about sources and amounts of income into the estate.

3. Ask the following questions:

• How many N.C. and federal estate returns would you estimate you have prepared?

• What is your charge per hour? What do you esti-

mate the total cost of this work to be?
• How long do you estimate the work will take?
• Will estimates be put in writing?

4. If you should have serious complaints about an accountant you hire, those complaints should be registered with the North Carolina State Board of Certified Public Accountant Examiners in Raleigh, 919-733-1422. This is the body that licenses accountants.

Appendix C

Account Options and Responsibilities

Though laws govern rights of surviving tenants, a financial institution's policies will influence the options available to you for handling funds in your care. This makes it impossible to say, "You always should...." or "You will always be able to...."

Your choices may also be influenced by the fact that employees sometimes have very limited understanding of their institution's policies covering estate accounts. Consequently, they may not be prepared to give you all the information you need.

Because of this, I suggest that you read this appendix, then contact each bank or other institution as soon as possible to ask questions related to your particular circumstances. Keep asking questions until you feel satisfied that you have discovered the best options available. If you feel confused or have questions that aren't being satisfactorily answered, don't make a decision until you have investigated further.

Some banks now have individuals or departments that specialize in such accounts. Always, however, there is a central office or someone, somewhere, with an authoritative word. Try to be sure that source is tapped.

Accounts in the Decedent's Name Only

1. Because the account holder has died, you may redeem a certificate of deposit without penalty before its maturity. There are some other accounts, too, that can be closed without a penalty.

2. If a beneficiary is due to get a net cash value that equals or exceeds the value of an account, you probably can have the account put into the beneficiary's name, if desired, with the same rate, yield, and maturity date as the decedent's account. You would not, of course, consider doing so unless those terms were better than currently available terms.

3. If there are investments you don't plan to redeem, sell, or transfer to beneficiaries right away, you may need to put the accounts into the estate's name. Interest and dividends earned after the decedent's death are estate income and are not supposed to be reported to the IRS under the decedent's tax ID (social security number). Talk with a knowledgeable employee about whether you need to put an account into the estate's name to enable the institution to report earnings under the estate's tax ID (the EIN).

Especially if total investments are going to earn enough to require filing a fiduciary return — an estate's version of the income tax return — the change to the estate's name may prevent complications with the IRS.

The IRS is apparently perfecting its ability to match income reported by financial institutions with that reported by individuals and estates on their returns. If what the institution reported under the decedent's social security number and what it reported under the estate's tax ID do not match what you report on the decedent's income tax return and the estate's fiduciary return, the resulting confusion can be difficult to untangle. As you talk with the institution's best advisors about whether to put an account into the estate's name, there are some other factors you should also consider.

a. If you change the account into the estate's name, will you be able to choose whether to retain the terms of the decedent's account? If currently available rates, yield, maturity dates, and other terms are better than those of the decedent's account, you would want to open the estate account with new terms. If, however, the terms agreed to by the decedent are better than currently available ones, you would want the estate account to retain the older terms.

I did not discover an institution unwilling to retain the terms of the decedent's account, but one said, "It's the bank's choice." If you are dealing with someone who says it isn't allowed, don't assume that person is an authority. If thorough investigation confirms that verdict, however, weigh the potential loss of earnings against potential confusion and hassle with the IRS.

b. If you change an account into the estate's name, will "ability to close before maturity without penalty" apply to the new account? Both my husband and I have had decedent's accounts put into an estate's name, with a new number, and later closed them before maturity without penalty. But if the institution you're dealing with cannot allow that, and if you are likely to need the funds before maturity, you will have to weigh the potential penalty against the potential problems with IRS.

c. Will putting the investment into the name of the estate alter the possibility of later transferring it to a beneficiary and allowing the beneficiary to retain the decedent's terms? One bank executive said, "bank's choice."

4. A checking account in the decedent's name must be closed and the funds put elsewhere if they are to be accessible. Such funds are often placed in an estate checking account. Before closing the decedent's account, be sure that all automatic deposits or withdrawals have been stopped.

5. Corporate stock and bond securities may be transferred to beneficiaries or sold so the value can be distributed or used for estate obligations. Some procedures require considerable time, so don't assume otherwise without inquiry. Ask whether putting an account into the estate's name may facilitate sale, especially if you want to sell soon.

Joint Accounts

1. For joint bank accounts created after June, 1989, defined by GS53-146, for which there is a valid right-of-survivorship signature card, the total funds go to the survivor and are not available to you. None of the account's value is considered a probate asset. (GS53-146 does seem to allow access to the property through GS28A-15-l0(a)(3) in certain cases of estate need.)

2. For joint accounts established under GS41-2.1, the statute makes the decedent's share available for your use for certain estate obligations — but only in

the event that all of certain assets have been exhausted. If those other assets have been exhausted, you may use the decedent's share of the GS41-2.1 account for paying the spouse's allowance, funeral expenses, administration costs, claims of creditors, governmental claims.

Any portion of the decedent's share which is not required within the statute's specifications must go to the surviving account holder. Some banks make the total account available to the surviving account holder, some put the decedent's share into the PR's hands. If you are responsible, meticulous records must assure the survivor his or her portion.

3. For joint accounts without right of survivorship, either statutory or common law, the decedent's share is part of the probate estate and totally available to you for your estate obligations.

4. Corporate stock and bond securities may be owned jointly with right of survivorship, but the decedent's interest in the account may still be liable for estate obligations. (GS41-2.2) Some sale or redemption procedures require considerable time, so don't delay inquiry.

From One Who's Been There

I have encountered several institutions' employees who did not understand the "no penalty for early closure" and did not understand the possibility of putting an account into the estate's name or a beneficiary's name and retaining its original terms. One bank manager, who also happened to be involved in the settlement of a relative's estate, said that even she had encountered some confusion related to accounts.

In two instances I had to go up two levels of authority before I found someone who understood and could properly direct the employee. That is awkward, but it can be done diplomatically by asking an employee to check with a supervisor or by requesting a copy of the institution's written policies for the handling of estate accounts.

Remember that policies and even laws can change, so either you or the person you deal with may be mistaken, but when there are different understandings, it's good to investigate further. If you are polite, neither you nor the employee need "lose face" if proven wrong. Remember, too, however, that your responsibility to protect the estate's money is more important than possible embarrassment and that in some cases penalties or lost earnings can mean a sizable loss.

In one case when I asked to see the policies, I was sent an inter-office memo which applied to other accounts but seemed to have nothing to do with estate accounts. A repeated request for actual policies, however, soon brought a letter saying, "We have decided to make an exception in your case."

It was not an exception. It was a discovery of the correct way to handle the matter. I know that because I called the head office and asked for an explanation of policies covering options for accounts after the death of the account holder. Without my asking anything more specific, I was told there was no penalty for early closure and that if the PR should choose to do so, the account could be put into a beneficiary's name and retain the original maturity date and original interest rate and yield.

Forms
and Where to Get Them

Even if you hire an accountant or a lawyer to file tax returns, your having copies of the forms and instructions may enable you to discover something of benefit to the estate and may facilitate communication between you and the one doing the returns.

From the N.C. Dept. of Revenue

(Pick them up, if there is an office near you, have an accountant get them, or order from Raleigh, 919-715-0397.)

For Decedent's Individual Income Tax:

Form D-400, "Individual Income Tax Return," for year(s) for which you are responsible. Year preceding death? Year of death?

Check the decedent's last filed returns to see if there are other N.C. income tax forms you are likely to need.

For Taxes Related to The Estate:

Form A-101, "N.C. Estate Tax Return," if necessary as explained in Guideline 17 (Instructions are on back).

Form D407, "Income Tax Return for Estates and Trusts," if necessary as explained in Guideline 20.

Publication D407A, "Instructions for D407" if it is

needed.

From the Internal Revenue Service

(Pick them up, if there is an office near you, or order by calling 1-800-829-3676, or have an accountant get them. You may also want their "Guide to Free Tax Services.")

For Decedent's Individual Income Tax:

Form 1040, "Individual Income Tax Return," for year(s) for which you are responsible. Year preceding year of death? Year of death?

Check the decedent's last-filed income tax return to see what other IRS forms you are likely to need.

Publication 17, "Your Federal Income Tax," instructions for filing the individual income tax return.

For Taxes Related to The Estate:

SS-4, "Application for Employer Identification Number." If you want the EIN in less than four weeks, get "Request Your Employer Identification Number by Phone" instructions.

Form 56, "Notice Concerning Fiduciary Relationship" — 2 copies, one for Guideline 13 and one for Guideline 25.

Publication 950, "Introduction to Estate and Gift Taxes," gives general information and explains when/how these taxes can be eliminated by the unified credit.

Publication 559, "Tax Information for Survivors, Executors, and Administrators."

Form 706, "United States Estate Tax Return," if needed as explained in Guideline 18.

Publication 448, "Federal Estate and Gift Taxes," instructions for filing estate and gift taxes if required.

Form 709, "United States Gift Tax Return" (see end of Guideline 18).

Form 1041, "U.S. Fiduciary Income Tax Return."

Publication 525, "Taxable and Non-taxable Income."

Schedule K-1 (Form 1041), one for each beneficiary, if needed.

Form 4810, "Request for Prompt Assessment," one for each return you file with IRS for which you want a limit set on the time they have in which to assess additional taxes.

Publication 559 and the "Guide to Free Tax Services" tell of other forms sometimes needed.

From the Clerk of Court

Application For Probate and Letters or Application for Letters of Administration.

Wording for Notice to Creditors

90-Day Inventory Form

Annual and/or Final Account Form(s)

Certified Copies of the Will

Tax Certification Form, AOC-E-212 or AOC-E207

Appendix E

Dispute Settlement

An estate involves property that has monetary and sentimental value. Since money and sentiment are common grounds for human conflict, an estate settlement offers possibilities for disagreements or disputes.

There are three dispute settlement processes recognized by our court system. They are mediation, arbitration and litigation. The first two have grown from an attempt to clear our courts of some of the backlog of cases that might be dealt with just as effectively, and perhaps with less loss of time and money, elsewhere.

If a dispute should arise, investigate to see which option best suits the circumstances.

The following represents my understanding of what was told me through phone interviews.

Mediation

Mediation is a process in which disagreeing parties come before a trained mediator and discuss their differences. Parties come with the intention of trying to reach an agreement that is mutually satisfactory, an agreement in which each "wins." If each is to win, of course, then each must be willing to negotiate, perhaps to "give" in some way.

If a decision is reached, the parties may choose to compose a memorandum of understanding. The memorandum will usually be only as binding as the honor the parties give to it.

There are 28 non-profit Mediation Network of North Carolina centers in our state. Because these are low-cost centers, they may not have mediators trained to work with every kind of dispute. Other options include individuals who work independently as mediators and other agencies that can put you in touch with a mediator. At the end of this section there is information about how to contact these resources.

Mediation services are the least costly of any of the dispute settlement options. They are either free or available at a small charge or on a sliding scale if arranged through one of the non-profit agencies. Costs cover a considerable range for independent mediators and other agencies.

Both parties may gain a great deal. They may find a solution that works for both, plus peaceful relationships and avoidance of costly settlement procedures.

Arbitration

Arbitration is a process in which disputing parties agree to come before one or more trained arbitrators, present their case and accept the ruling. The decision made by arbitrators is legally binding. The way it will be binding is clarified and agreed upon before the process begins. In some situations, the ruling is binding on both parties. In some, the ruling is binding on one party only. For example, if one of the parties is a lawyer, some arbitration panels make the ruling binding on an attorney but not on the other party.

Costs will vary according to the case and the arbitrator hired. There are independent arbitrators and some agencies.

Litigation

Litigation is a process in which there is a contest conducted through the court system, usually with lawyers representing the disputing parties.

One party wins, the other loses. The judgment, reached through due process of the court system, is binding on both parties.

The costs depend on attorneys' fees, court costs, length of time involved, etc.

How To Decide

As far as I can determine, all the sources of help discussed above are willing to give free information and answers to questions that will help you determine whether their service is what you need.

You will want to be sure you understand the potential outcomes and the costs and what they cover.

Before the process begins, you should get a written statement of costs or at least a written estimate.

You should also learn about the training and experience of those who will mediate, arbitrate or litigate. Ask for references and talk with those persons. If you are hiring a lawyer, read Appendix B of this book.

How To Reach
The Above-Mentioned Agencies

To find the non-profit agencies, look in the yellow pages of your telephone directory under "Mediation Services" or under "Dispute Settlement Services," or call directory assistance. Some of these services also have other names. In Greensboro, for instance, it is "One Step Further," but they are also listed in the directory under "Mediation Services." If there is not such an agency in your town, you may call the one in Greensboro and ask for the name and location of the agency nearest you.

To find names of independent mediators/arbitrators, or other agencies, look in the yellow pages under Mediation Services or Arbitration Services; call the courthouse and see if you can learn of court recommendations; check attorneys' advertisements to see if they do that type of work.

Resources

To read the North Carolina laws that relate to estate settlement procedures, go to your library and ask where to find the General Statutes. In some libraries, they are in the North Carolina section. In others, they may be found in the general research area.

You will find most of the laws related to your work in Volume 7, which contains chapters 28-41, of the *General Statutes of North Carolina*, Prepared under the Supervision of The Department of Justice of the State of North Carolina, The Michie Co., Law Publishers, Charlottesville, Va., 1990.

You will, however, find banking and tax laws and some other pertinent statutes in other volumes. Subjects and chapters are on volumes' spines.

If you read statutes, you MUST BE SURE to check the supplement inserted in the front or back of the book to see if the law you're interested in has been amended or repealed. Numbers identifying amendments match the laws in the main text of a volume. (Reading case notes also often helps clarify a law. You may also be assisted by referring to the User's Guide near the beginning of Volume 1.)

Remember that there may be several laws, some of which you do not know about, that have some bearing on particular circumstances. In other words, while all of us should be more familiar with the laws and will find reading them helpful, a lawyer's training makes him or her likely to be able to gain a more complete picture of possibilities and a fuller understanding of implications for individual situations.

The books below helped me to identify pertinent statutes and, hopefully, to better understand what I was being told by lawyers, clerks and others. They contain much additional clarification of laws and estate settlement procedures.

North Carolina Will Drafting and Probate Practice Handbook, Revised Edition — 1990, Wake Forest University School of Law.

N.C. Probate Handbook, by Mark B. Edwards, The Harrison Co., Publishers, 3110 Crossing Park, Norcross, Ga. 30071, 1982, 1994. (Check to see if a supplement is inserted.)

Wills and Administration of Estates in N. C., second and third editions, Norman A. Wiggins, Volumes I & II, The Harrison Co., Publishers, 3110 Crossing Park, Norcross, Ga. 30071, 1983, 1993. (A supplement is probably inserted.)

Law information from any book other than the General Statutes should be checked against the statutes, remembering to check the supplement to see if laws have been amended.

How to Deal
With Your Own
Estate Now

Your work with the settlement of an estate has perhaps made you intensely aware of the value of good planning and the need for re-evaluating your own provisions for a time when you may not be able to speak for yourself. While recent experience and new knowledge can provide incentive and guidance, the following suggestions may help you translate good intentions into responsible action.

A Checklist

_____**1.** Look at your property in the light of how it will be transferred to survivors if left as it is now. Determine whether there are changes you want to make.

Scan Chapter 5 to see how property will be distributed if your instructions for it are not clearly specified in a legal document. Possibilities include its being divided with minor children or parents, guardians being appointed by the court to manage assets awarded to minors, and a large portion of it being unavailable to a spouse.

There are several ways to assure that your property is distributed according to your wishes. The most appropriate and effective choices depend, to a considerable extent, on the size of your estate.

You must determine whether your estate is large enough (or likely to become large enough) to be subject to federal and N.C. estate taxes. If the gross value of the estate of a single person — or the gross value of a married couple's combined assets — is greater than the amount excluded from N.C. and federal estate taxes (see Guideline 17), you need to seek professional guidance to explore strategies that can minimize the taxable estate and possibly save your estate many, many thousands of dollars. The establishment of one of several kinds of trusts is currently a popular and effective minimizing strategy, and some trusts also allow the bypassing of much of the probate process.

When determining the gross value of your estate, you must include land and buildings (less mortgages and liens), bank accounts and investments, life insurance with you as "owner" or the estate as beneficiary, certain annuities, and the value of certain property if it's transferred within 3 years before your death. There are several allowable deductions, but your estate may still be worth more, when viewed through the government's eyes, than you realize. If there is even a possibility your estate's value will exceed the exclusion amount, don't delay making an appointment with a qualified estate planner, trust officer, tax specialist, financial planner or attorney specializing in estate planning. The professional can guide you concerning the relationship of a will to whatever other strategy is recommended, but a will, alone, will not minimize taxability.

If you do not need the above, you do need a will that covers all assets other than properties which have contracts you've worded so that they pass directly to beneficiaries and, thus, bypass probate. (Such non-probate properties may include real estate, annuities, life insurance, right-of-survivorship accounts, etc. Be aware that some of these assets are not totally immune to estate debts and claims. You may also want to consider that if both parties of a right-of-survivorship contract should die at the same time, the wishes of both are negated unless secondary beneficiaries are named.)

_____**2.** Make or update your will and/or your trust to assure the honoring of your wishes for all property.

Learn all you can about wills and trusts. You may well need or prefer a combination of the two. There is considerable written material available, and lawyers and estate or financial planners are often willing to give free programs to groups.

Have your will and/or trust drawn by an attorney. Do-it-yourself documents can bequeath many headaches to those you care about. (If finances are a problem, contact your local Legal Aid Society. If you can't locate that number, call their central office in Raleigh: Legal Services of N.C., 919-856-2564. If you are 60 or older, check with Legal Aid if you would like one of their attorneys to draw your will free of charge.

You may also want to ask your Council on Aging or Older Adult Services of your Department of Social Services about possible funds for having your will done elsewhere.

Before going to the attorney, make a list of your real property and personal property (see No. 6 for some reminders) and the individuals or organizations you would like to receive those assets. Consider where you would like a beneficiary's share to go in the event the beneficiary pre-deceases you or dies before having received the total benefit due. After specific bequests, consider where you want the residuary to go. All to one person? A percentage to each of several?

Discuss the above with your lawyer so he or she can help you think of all aspects that should be considered.

Be sure to designate someone to care for any dependent children.

If you are married, both you and your spouse should have your own will (and trust?) and should be sure that your individual wishes are adequately and accurately expressed.

If there are items, even "insignificant" ones, that you want to be absolutely sure are transferred to particular individuals, include them in a legal document.

Don't choose an executor for a will solely because of kinship or friendship. Consider capability. If a business is involved, also consider familiarity with it, or perhaps designate an advisor and compensation for that person. A bank or trust company may be appointed executor or co-executor with one or more individuals if that seems wise. If you consider this, carefully investigate costs.

If you already have a will, review and update it. Be sure it's self-proving, a fairly new legal arrangement that relieves the executor of having to track down witnesses and have them verify their signatures. If the will was drawn by an attorney, the witnesses' signatures notarized and an affidavit attached, the will is self-proving. Be sure it still accurately reflects your wishes. An old will may name persons now deceased, may not express changed thinking.

If you make a new will, destroy the old one or write across it the date and location of the new will.

Put the original and a copy of the will or trust document in separate, safe places. (Consider that if a bank lockbox is wholly or partially in the deceased's name, its contents can't be removed until the box is inventoried by a qualified person. See Guideline 2.) Make a note of the location of both the original and the copy and put that note in the file recommended in suggestion 5 below, or put one of the documents in that file and note the location of the other.

_____**3.** Consider living accommodations for yourself in the event of disability and consider options available to your survivors in the event of your death. Are you planning toward a retirement center or nursing facility and, if so, have you found out about costs, how far in advance of entry you must apply, etc.?

Would a surviving spouse need to move to less expensive accommodations? If there are minor children, what would be the options if both you and your spouse should die? Are there relatives with whom they can live or might a children's home be the best viable option?

_____**4.** Authorize someone to act for you when you are unable to assume responsibility.

a. Give someone a durable power of attorney to act in your behalf in the event you are temporarily or permanently disabled. The power of attorney will assure that bills can be paid, tax returns filed, other business and legal matters taken care of. This can be of enormous help to you and others while you are still living and, by enabling someone to keep affairs in order, it will also benefit your estate. Be sure that the POA is a "durable" power of attorney, one that will avoid possible necessity of court procedure to declare you incompetent in order for someone to act in your behalf. This document must be drawn by a lawyer. It can then be filed with the Register of Deeds when and if there is need to activate it.

b. Obtain, properly complete, and put into the appropriate hands the advance directives that state your wishes for your care in the event you become unable to make such decisions for yourself. Putting your wishes in writing can provide considerable peace of mind for you as well as for those who could, otherwise, have to make those choices for you. Current options include:

(1) the Health Care Power of Attorney, in which you name someone to make medical care decisions for you;

(3) The Living Will, in which you state your desire to die a natural death if you are terminally and incurably sick or in a persistent vegetative state.

(3) the Advance Instruction for Mental Health Treatment, in which you tell doctors and health care providers what mental health treatments you would and would not want.

Laws will probably continue to change in relation to these matters. Consequently, it is not wise to pick up a form from just anywhere. Forms and instructions that reflect new laws are available at reputable hospitals and nursing homes. All these forms require witnesses; the first two must also be notarized. Before signing these forms, you may want to discuss concerns with your physician as well as with family members.

_____**5.** Prepare a file folder or large manila envelope with a caption such as Death/Serious Illness. Be sure responsible family members, probably all adult children, know the location of this file. Update the file at least once a year.

In this folder or envelope, place inventories and other papers referred to on these pages — or make a list of locations for all the documents and place the list in this file. Also note location of the lockbox, if there is one, and location of lockbox keys.

File notes you would want passed on to your children's guardian in the event of the death of both parents: doctors' names; the children's allergies/other physical problems; their special likes/dislikes, even bedtime rituals, anything that might make transition easier.

File notes that the surviving spouse would find helpful if suddenly left with responsibilities now shouldered by you: car care, finances, communication with children's school, doctors, counselors, etc.

_____**6.** Make two lists.

List No. 1: An inventory of your property and major liabilities. List all accounts, real estate, pension program, insurance, other investments, automobiles, valuable collections, etc. Give the name of banks or other financial institutions, account numbers, names on accounts. Give approximate values (note the date) for each asset. Unless you are using a computer and can easily edit, you may want to write dates and values in pencil to simplify annual update.

If you group property according to joint ownership with right of survivorship, joint ownership without right of survivorship, and property in your name only, you will get a very helpful perspective of your estate and a perspective that may assist you as you make changes or additions. List all major liabilities such as mortgages, loans, any other long-term debts such as for a car. Give the name of the institution or individual to whom the debt is owed and the account number. Note the date and approximate amount still owed.

List No. 2: Household and personal items you would like to go to specific individuals. Though not legally binding, such a listing can be very helpful to survivors who are willing to honor it. Also write down information you want preserved about those or other items you own, such as that a particular bowl was handed down from a great grandparent. Otherwise, such information may be lost forever.

_____**7.** Go to your bank.

Check on signature cards for any joint accounts; be sure the contracts reflect your wishes so far as right of survivorship is concerned. Be sure that both parties' signatures actually appear on signature cards. Bank signature cards are, since 1989, right-of-survivorship cards, but right of survivorship is not available unless both parties do actually sign.

Note: If a spouse becomes terminally ill without signing such a card and the other feels she or he would need access to the total funds in the event of death, the funds should be moved into a personal account before the death occurs.

If you have a jointly held lockbox, label contents according to ownership. This will clarify what must be listed as property of the one who dies first.

_____**8.** Encourage each adult family member to establish credit in his or her own name. This is most often done by:

(1) making significant purchases (house, car, etc.) and making consistently prompt payment.

(2) having a credit card and keeping a good credit rating by consistently prompt payments. If cards are in joint names, have credit records established for each individual named on the card by (a) listing both, on the application, as liable parties, or (b) by phoning your request.

_____**9.** Let your wishes be known in relation to organ donorship, cremation or burial, funeral service, other details.

If you want to donate organs, make those arrangements.

If you want to be cremated rather than buried,

investigate details, with the funeral home, and file instructions. Note your wishes concerning what to do with ashes. Explain your thinking to close family members. If you fail to do this so they can adjust to the idea, they may feel robbed of ritual important to their grieving and adjustment.

If burial is your preference, secure plots.

Become more observant of ways in which funeral homes' services differ. Some offer considerably more services, some give more personal attention, some offer free grief counseling and support groups. Decide which you prefer.

Consider whether you want to purchase a pre-need contract through the funeral home to enable arrangements to be made and paid for, or payment begun, ahead of time. Study contracts very carefully. Some are good but some are rip-offs. Make notes concerning music requests or any other wishes related to your funeral service. Also make notes about anything you would want mentioned in a news article. When survivors are numb with grief, even important information may not come to mind.

_____**10.** Review, and if possible have a qualified person review with you, your overall plans for financial security for yourself if you should become disabled. Also review plans for financial security of your survivors.

Get a print-out from social security that clarifies what your benefits would be, based on your record at this point. Get a copy of the social security booklet, 'Survivors." It tells of the small lump-sum death benefit for a surviving spouse and the benefits available for minors until age 18 or 19 if they are full-time elementary or secondary students. It also clarifies the ages at which certain percentages can be drawn on one's own record or on a spouse's record.

Determine approximate monthly amount that could be available from your investments, insurance, any retirement or disability benefits and social security.

Use the information to aid your ongoing plan for your own and your family's security and to put your estate in order for those who will handle it after your death.

If, or when, someone who is dear to you becomes responsible for your business affairs, your medical care, your funeral and your estate, that person will be deeply grateful for — and greatly assisted by — any time and effort you give the ten steps suggested in this chapter.